4/04

D0044146

THE War ON THE Bill of Rights

and the Gathering Resistance

THE War ON THE Bill of Rights

and the Gathering Resistance

NAT HENTOFF

SEVEN STORIES PRESS

New York · London · Toronto · Melbourne

Seven Stories Press
140 Watts Street
New York, NY 10013
www.sevenstories.com

In Canada: Hushion House, 36 Northline Road, Toronto, Ontario M4B 3E2

In the U.K.: Turnaround Publisher Services Ltd., Unit 3, Olympia Trading Estate,
Coburg Road, Wood Green, London N22 6TZ

In Australia: Palgrave Macmillan, 627 Chapel Street, South Yarra VIC 3141

College professors may order examination copies of Seven Stories Press titles for a free
six-month trial period. To order, visit www.sevenstories.com/textbook/, or fax on
school letterhead to 212.226.1411.

LIBRARY OF CONGRESS CATALOGING-IN-PUBLICATION DATA
Hentoff, Nat.
  The war on the Bill of Rights—and the gathering resistance / Nat
Hentoff.— 1st ed.
    p. cm.
  ISBN 1-58322-621-4 (alk. paper)
  1. Civil rights—United States. 2. Dissenters—United States. 3.
Government, Resistance to—United States. 4. United States—Politics
and government—2001- 5. War on Terrorism, 2001- I. Title.
JC599.U45 H46 2003
323.4'9'0973—dc21

                              2003014162

9 8 7 6 5 4 3 2 1

Printed in the USA.

This book's call to preserve and protect the Bill of Rights is dedicated to Samuel Adams (1722–1803). He was instrumental in forming Boston's Committee of Correspondence and encouraged the formation of other informational committees throughout the colonies. His "declaration of rights," adopted by the Boston Committee of Correspondence, helped create the climate for the Declaration of Independence.

Contents

We will not allow this enemy to win the war by changing our way of life or restricting our freedoms.

—President George W. Bush, September 12, 2001

We're not sacrificing civil liberties. We're securing civil liberties.

—Attorney General John Ashcroft, September 11, 2002

What is more startling than the scope of these new powers is that the government can use them on people who aren't suspected of committing a crime. Innocent people can be deprived of any clue that they are being watched and that they may need to defend themselves.

—Lincoln Caplan, editor, *Legal Affairs*, Yale University

Power makes men wanton . . . It intoxicates the mind.

—Sam Adams, signer of the Declaration of Independence, *Boston Gazette*, 1771

The spirit of resistance to government is so valuable on certain occasions, that I wish it to be always kept alive . . . The People are the only sure reliance for the preservation of our liberty.

—Thomas Jefferson

Congress of the United States,

Begun and held at the City of New York, on
Wednesday the fourth of March, one thousand seven hundred and eighty nine.

THE

RESOLVED

ARTICLES

CHAPTER ONE

"Why Should We Care? It's Only the Constitution"

In a September 2002 Century Foundation report, *The Enemy Within: Intelligence Gathering, Law Enforcement, and Civil Liberties in the Wake of September 11*, New York University law professor Stephen J. Schulhofer said of the national security regulations then in place—with more to come—some "compromise important freedoms in ways that previous presidents never attempted, even in the midst of formally declared wars. And important changes in the law have been adopted by the Department of Justice unilaterally, without public input or congressional approval."

This erosion of sections of the Bill of Rights began to be quickened when the president signed the USA PATRIOT Act on October 26, 2001. With Attorney General John Ashcroft insisting on the crucial need for speed, the House passed the 342-page document by a vote of 356 to 66, although few had had the chance to read it. Several members later said that parts of the new law seemed unconstitutional, but in view of the coming elections, they did not want to be attacked as "unpatriotic" by their opponents. In the Senate, only one senator, Wisconsin's Russ Feingold, voted against the USA PATRIOT Act.

In the House, dissenter David Obey of Wisconsin said bitterly, "Why should we care? It's only the Constitution."

The Act has radically extended government electronic surveillance—on and off the Internet—with often reduced judicial review. For example, FBI agents can enter a home or office with a court order—while the occupants are not there—and insert the "Magic Lantern" (also known as the keystroke logger) into a computer.

It records every stroke, including messages not ever sent from the computer. On returning covertly, the agents can download everything that has been recorded. Notice of their entry can be delayed for ninety days or longer. More on this as we go on.

Also, under the USA PATRIOT Act, with a warrant from the secret Foreign Intelligence Surveillance Court, the FBI is empowered to go to libraries and bookstores to secure the lists of books borrowed or bought by persons under only tenuous suspicion of links to terrorism. A much lower standard than the Fourth Amendment's "probable cause" is permitted for these inquiries.

Furthermore, under a gag rule unprecedented in American history, both the librarian and the bookstore owner are prohibited from informing anyone, including the press, that these searches have taken place. There will be further details—and resistance to this Ashcroft invasion of privacy—in a following chapter.

Among the extraordinary unilateral incursions in the Bill of Rights taken by John Ashcroft: government agents can now listen in on conversations between lawyers and their clients in federal prisons without a prior court order. And there is the designation of two American citizens, so far, as "enemy combatants," held in military brigs in this country, without charges and without access to lawyers, and unable to appear personally in court hearings. They are being held indefinitely for interrogation about their possible knowledge of or links to terrorism.

In the case of Yaser Hamdi, taken into custody in Afghanistan and now in a Virginia navy brig, Federal District Judge Robert Doumar, a Reagan appointee, has asked the Justice Department lawyer, "So the Constitution doesn't apply to Mr. Hamdi?" This treatment of American citizens, Judge Doumar has said, "appears to be the first in American jurisprudence." According to an August 8, 2002, *Wall Street Journal* news report—which John Ashcroft's office has not denied—there are plans for more such indefinite detentions of alleged American "enemy combatants" without charges or access to lawyers.

Since the Hamdi case is crucial to an understanding of the Justice Department's attacks on our most fundamental liberties, it will be fully explored in chapter 10.

For some time after September 11, polls and other indications showed that a considerable majority of the citizenry agreed that the real prospect that terrorist enemies were plotting actions within this country indeed required a diminishing of civil liberties—and were willing to sacrifice their liberties for security.

But, in the *Federalist Papers* (47) James Madison had warned: "The accumulation of all powers, legislative, executive, and judiciary, in the same hands, whether of one, a few, or many, may justly be pronounced the very definition of tyranny." Even if the *Federalist Papers* were familiar to much of the citizenry, it did not appear for months that this alarm by a principal architect of the Constitution would have disquieted them, even though the president and his attorney general were rapidly accumulating power unto themselves.

But with more Americans beginning to realize that the Bush-Ashcroft revisions of the constitutional rule of law apply not only to immigrants but also to citizens, resistance began to rise in various parts of the country. Even in the previously compliant Congress, Wisconsin's James Sensenbrenner, a conservative Republican, objected strenuously to Ashcroft's loosening of FBI surveillance guidelines—allowing agents to covertly attend and monitor public meetings, as well as mosques and other church services, without any prior specific leads. Sensenbrenner said he did not want us to go back to "the bad old days when the FBI was spying on people like Martin Luther King."

Another conservative Republican, Dick Armey, the House majority leader, struck out of the markup of the administration's bill setting up a Department of Homeland Security, a provision called "Operation TIPS." This Justice Department plan would have enlisted millions of deliverymen, truckers, service workers, and other Americans with access to our homes and offices—to report on any "suspicious" talk or activities. There was no definition of "suspicious." Armey refused, he said, to allow a law enabling "Americans to spy on other Americans." Congress finally rejected Operations TIPS, but Ashcroft keeps trying to bring it back.

Even soon after September 11, there were initial signs of a broad range of resisters. In trying to influence the Congressional vote on the USA PATRIOT Act, the American Civil Liberties Union organized a coalition across the ideological spectrum from Phyllis Schlafly's Eagle Forum to People for the American Way to the National Rifle Association. Also included were the Arab-American Anti-Discrimination Committee, the Center for Constitutional Rights, the Free Congress Foundation, the NAACP Board of Directors, the Baptist Joint Committee on Public Affairs, and Amnesty International USA.

By September 2002, retired Army General Wesley Clark, former commander of Allied forces in Kosovo, was saying on National Public Radio that we are engaged in a "prolonged struggle" against terrorism, but this is not the kind of war that demands "we can't pay attention to the ordinary processes of government. It's the opposite. This is the kind of war that demands we pay *more* attention to our rights as citizens."

On the same NPR program, Andy Kohut, director of the Pew Center for Research, noted that while Americans after September 11 were ready to trade liberties for security, more recent surveys showed that more of us were becoming apprehensive about those compromises.

And in the heartland—Fort Wayne, Indiana—the *Daily Journal Gazette*, three days before the first anniversary of September 11, published an indictment of Ashcroft and the Bush administration in an editorial, "Attacks on Liberty." It was the paper's first full-page editorial in nearly twenty years. The *Journal Gazette* charged:

> In the name of national security, President Bush, Attorney General John Ashcroft, and even Congress have pulled strand after strand out of the constitutional fabric that distinguishes the United States from other nations . . .
>
> Actions taken over the past year are eerily reminiscent of tyranny portrayed in the most nightmarish works of fiction. The power to demand reading lists from libraries could have been drawn from the pages of Ray Bradbury's *Fahrenheit 451* . . . The sudden suspension of due process

for immigrants rounded up into jails is familiar to readers of Sinclair Lewis's *It Can't Happen Here.*

Among the quotations from distinguished Americans in the editorial was one of my favorites—Louis Brandeis's "The greatest dangers to liberty lurk in insidious encroachment by men of zeal,
well-meaning but without understanding."

The most remarkable surge of grassroots resistance—though
hardly remarked yet by most of the media—is the formation of Bill
of Rights Defense Committees, which began in Northampton, Massachusetts, in February 2002.

Twenty-five teachers, retirees, doctors, lawyers, nurses, and students formed the first Bill of Rights Defense Committee in order to
protect the residents of the town from the USA PATRIOT Act and the
stream of unilateral abuses of the Constitution by the attorney general. Their action, soon to be replicated in scores of other towns and
cities, harkened back to the pre-revolutionary Committees of Correspondence, initiated by Sam Adams and others of the Sons of Liberty in Boston in 1767.

In 1805, Mercy Otis Warren—in her *History of the Rise and
Progress and Termination of the American Revolutions,* emphasized:
"Perhaps no single step contributed so much to cement the union
of the colonies, and the final acquisition of independence, as the
establishment of the Committees of Correspondence . . . that produced unanimity and energy throughout the continent." These
patriots spread the news throughout the colonies about such
British subversions of fundamental liberties as the general search
warrant that gave British customs officers free reign to invade
homes and offices in pursuit of contraband. Justice William Brennan once told me that, in his reading of American history, those
horror stories of Americans and their goods being turned upside
down were indeed a key precipitating cause of the American
Revolution.

By May 2, the Northampton City Council unanimously passed
a resolution to protect the liberties of its citizens by mandating
local police agencies to inform the town when the agents of

Ashcroft were implementing the USA PATRIOT Act in Northampton and its environs.

Since then, such committees in more than 130 cities, towns, and counties in twenty-five states—and the legislatures of three entire states—have passed or are working on resolutions similar to those inaugurated by the original Bill of Rights Defense Committee. And, in another grassroots operation, the Japanese-American Bar Association in California—remembering the detention of Japanese-Americans during the Second World War that was approved by the Supreme Court—have organized a community group in Little Tokyo, Los Angeles. Reported by the *Los Angeles Daily Journal*, a newspaper covering legal affairs, the group "hopes, through community outreach and community forums, to help make people aware of the civil rights (and liberties) abuses that can result as a backlash to acts of terrorism."

In Ann Arbor, Michigan, where an active Bill of Rights Defense Committee had been functioning for months, City Councilwoman Heidi Herrell told ABC *News Online*: "At times like these, I think our constitutional rights are even more important. There have been times when we relaxed these things—the McCarthy era . . . and the detention of Japanese-Americans in World War II. We look back at those times with shame . . . I think this will be another time we look back with shame. That's what I fear."

But still not widely recognized is whether there will be time to look back to restore our liberties. In *The Enemy Within*, Stephen Schulhofer notes that "The Patriot Act includes a 'sunset' provision, so that certain new powers will lapse if not re-enacted by the end of 2005. But many of the most significant statutory changes are exempted from this proviso and will remain in effect indefinitely." (Such as the "Magic Lantern"; and the lowering of judicial review in surveillance and searches that apply not only to foreign intelligence but are now a regular part of criminal investigations.)

And, as I will detail, the administration is planning far more assaultive legislation on the Bill of Rights. Furthermore, as New York University law professor Burt Neuborne pointed out on Bill Moyers's public television program *Now*:

What really differentiates this period from past periods when the Constitution has been bent is that each of the past periods had a finite opening and a finite closing. The kind of threat we face now is open-ended from a time standpoint. [This is] international terrorism launched against us by ideologues, by small groups of ideologues. We're never going to see the end of that. And so, unlike the past incidents, if we do damage to our Constitutional heritage now, it isn't temporary.

And as this war on terrorism continues, young Americans will have become accustomed to—indeed conditioned to—the diminishment of the Bill of Rights.

They are less likely to think of lost liberties, never having experienced those liberties. Thurgood Marshall—in his dissenting opinion in *Skinner v. Railway Labor Executives' Association* (1989), prophesied our present danger:

> History teaches that grave threats to liberty often come in times of urgency, when constitutional rights seem too extravagant to endure. The World War II relocation cases, and the Red Scare and McCarthy-era internal subversion cases, are only the most extreme reminders that when we allow fundamental freedoms to be sacrificed in the name of real or perceived exigency, we invariably come to regret it.

But we can no longer be sure how much liberty future generations will have known to regret its disappearance. On September 12, 2002, Martín Espada—a poet, lawyer, and professor at the University of Massachusetts in Amherst—said on the Jim Lehrer *Newshour*. "Ultimately, Osama bin Laden cannot restrict our civil liberties. Only we can do that to ourselves.

"Al-Qaeda can not take away our freedoms. Only we can do that to ourselves . . . The only way the essential character of this country will change is if we permit it to change."

Meanwhile, the December 20, 2002, *New York Times* reported, "the Bush administration is planning to propose requiring Internet service providers to help build a centralized system to enable broad monitoring of the *Internet and, potentially, surveillance of its users through the Internet.*" (Emphasis added.)

CHAPTER TWO

How We Began to
Lose Our Liberties

As I reported in the *Village Voice* and *The Progressive*, in November 2001: two nights after the September 11 attack, the Senate swiftly, by voice vote after thirty minutes of debate, attached to a previously written appropriations bill an amendment making it much easier for the government to wiretap computers of terrorism suspects without having to go to various courts to get multiple search warrants. The bipartisan bill was introduced by Senators Orrin Hatch, Republican of Utah, and Dianne Feinstein, Democrat of California. "Terrorism" was not defined.

That was the beginning of the steamroller. Attorney General John Ashcroft then got his way with his originally titled Anti-Terrorism Act of 2001, which coolly contradicted the earnest assertions of the president and the secretary of defense that necessary security measures would not violate our fundamental liberties because our freedom is what we are fighting for. The final legislation passed the Senate on October 25 by a vote of 98 to 1, with only Russ Feingold, Democrat of Wisconsin, dissenting. In the House, the bill passed 356 to 66.

The law permits government agents to search a suspect's home without immediately notifying the object of the search. In J. Edgar Hoover's day, this was known as a "black bag job." The FBI then never bothered to get a search warrant for such operations. Now, a warrant would be required, but very few judges would turn a government investigator down in this time of fear. Ashcroft's "secret searches" provision can now extend to *all* criminal cases and can include taking photographs, the contents of your hard drive, and other property. This is now a permanent part of the law, not subject to any "sunset" review by Congress.

Ashcroft also asked for roving wiretaps—a single warrant for a suspect's telephone must include any and all types of phones he or she uses in any and all locations, including pay phones. If a suspect uses a relative's phone or your phone, that owner becomes part of the investigative database. So does anyone using the same pay phone or any pay phone in the area.

Ashcroft neglected to tell us, however, that roving wiretaps already became law under the Clinton Administration in 1998. At that time, only Congressman Bob Barr, Republican of Georgia, spoke against it in Congress, while the media paid little attention to this revision of the Fourth Amendment.

But Ashcroft demanded and received a radical extension of these roving wiretaps: a one-stop *national* warrant for wiretapping these peripatetic phones. Until now, a wiretap warrant was valid only in the jurisdiction in which it was issued. But now, the government won't have to waste time by having to keep going to court to provide a basis for each warrant in each locale.

The expansion of wiretapping to computers, and thereby the Internet, makes a mockery of Internet champion John Perry Barlow's 1996 "Declaration of the Independence of Cyberspace":

> Governments of the industrial world, on behalf of the future, I ask you of the past to leave us alone.... You have no sovereignty where we gather ... nor do you possess any methods of enforcement we have true reason to fear. Cyberspace does not lie within your borders.

This government invasion of cyberspace fulfills the prophecy of Justice Louis Brandeis, who warned, in his dissent in the first wiretapping case before the Supreme Court, *Olmstead v. United States* (1928), "Ways may some day be developed by which the Government, without removing papers from secret drawers, can reproduce them in court, and by which it will be enabled to expose to a jury the most intimate occurrences of the home."

This has come to pass. The government now has access to bank records, credit card purchases, what has been searched for on the Internet, and a great deal more data from those who have "supported," or are suspected of, terrorism.

Moreover, as Brandon Koerner, a fellow at the New America Foundation, has pointed out in the *Village Voice*, the bill that Congress passed so hastily on the night of September 13—and that is now part of the law—"lowers the legal standards necessary for the FBI to deploy its infamous Carnivore surveillance system." Without showing—as the Fourth Amendment requires—probable cause that a crime has been committed or is about to be committed, the government invades your privacy through Carnivore.

The fearful name "Carnivore" disturbed some folks, and so it has been renamed DCS1000. Carnivore, Koerner notes, is "a computer that the Feds attach to an Internet service provider. Once in place, it scans e-mail traffic for 'suspicious' subjects which, in the current climate, could be something as innocent as a message with the word 'Allah' in the header." Or maybe: "SAVE THE FOURTH AMENDMENT FROM TYRANTS!" Carnivore also records other electronic communications.

There was resistance to the assault on the Bill of Rights. In Congress, such previously unlikely alliances between Maxine Waters and Bob Barr, Barney Frank and Dick Armey, helped hold back Ashcroft's rush to enact his antiterrorism weapons within a week, as he had demanded. In the Senate, Patrick Leahy, chairman of the Judiciary Committee, also tried to allow some deliberation, but Majority Leader Tom Daschle usurped and undermined Leahy's authority. Leahy ultimately caved and declared the law signed by Bush on October 26 "a good bill that protects our liberties."

The House Judiciary Committee did pass by a 36-to-0 vote a bipartisan bill that restored some mention of the Bill of Rights to Ashcroft's proposals. But, late at night, that bill was scuttled behind closed doors by Speaker of the House Dennis Hastert and other Republican leaders, along with emissaries from the White House.

As a result, on October 12, the House, 337 to 39, approved a harsh bill that most of its members had not had time even to read. David Dreier, chairman of the Committee on Rules, often seen being smoothly disingenuous on television, said casually that it was hardly the first time bills had been passed that House members had not read.

Democrat David Obey of Wisconsin accurately described the maneuver as "a back-room quick fix."

And Barney Frank made the grim point that this subversion of representative government was "the least democratic process for debating questions fundamental to democracy I have ever seen. A bill drafted by a handful of people in secret, subject to no committee process, comes before us immune from amendment."

Among those voting against the final bill were Barney Frank, John Conyers, David Bonior, Barbara Lee, Cynthia McKinney, John Dingell, Jesse Jackson Jr., Jerrold Nadler, Melvin Watt, and Maxine Waters. Unaccountably, Bob Barr voted for the bill.

But House Judiciary Committee Chairman James Sensenbrenner, as reported on National Public Radio, assured us all that this steamrollered bill did not diminish the freedom of "innocent citizens."

Providing, of course, that the presumption of innocence holds. (Sensenbrenner was later to change his mind.)

Also late at night, on October 11, the Senate, in a closed-door session attended only by Senate leaders and members of the Administration, created a similar, expansive antiterrorism bill that the Senate went on to pass by a vote of ninety-six to one. Only Russ Feingold, a Wisconsin Democrat, had the truly patriotic courage to vote against this attack on the Bill of Rights that the president and the secretaries of state and defense have said we are fighting for.

As Feingold had said while the Senate was allegedly deliberating the bill, "It is crucial that civil liberties in this country be preserved. Otherwise I'm afraid terror will win this battle without firing a shot."

In essence, the new law will, as the *Wall Street Journal* noted, "make it easier for government agents to track e-mail sent and Web sites visited by someone involved in an investigation; to collect call records for phones such a person might use; and to share information between the Federal Bureau of Investigation and the Central Intelligence Agency."

Until now, the CIA was not legally allowed to spy on Americans. Also, previously secret grand jury proceedings will now be shared among law enforcement and intelligence agencies.

In addition, the new law subverts the Fourth Amendment's standards of reasonable searches and seizures by allowing antiterrorism investigations to obtain a warrant not on the basis of previously defined "probable cause," as has been required in domestic criminal probes, but on the much looser basis that the information is "relevant to an ongoing criminal investigation" somehow linked to alleged terrorism.

The new law has a "sunset clause," requiring it to be reviewed in December 2005, to determine if these stringent measures are still needed. But before this collusion in reducing our liberties was effected, George W. Bush had assured us that the war on worldwide terrorism will be of indeterminate length. A Congress that so overwhelmingly passed this antiterrorism bill is hardly likely to expunge parts of it unless there is rising citizen resistance. And even if it did, evidence gathered in the first four years could be used in prosecutions after that. Moreover, not every part of the PATRIOT ACT is subject to the sunset clause. There are sections that are now part of our permanent laws.

In self-defense, all of us should be interested in how terrorism is defined in this historic legislation. As summarized by the ACLU, the language in the final bill said: A person "commits the crime of domestic terrorism if within the U.S., activity is engaged in that involves acts dangerous to human life that violate the laws of the United States or any State, and appear to be intended to: (1) intimidate or coerce a civilian population; (2) influence the policy of a government by intimidation or coercion; or (3) affect the conduct of the government by mass destruction, assassination, or kidnapping." (Note the words: "appear to be intended to" and "intimidate.")

Considering the loose language of the first two provisions, the ACLU points out that "this over-broad terrorism definition would sweep in people who engage in acts of political protest if those acts were dangerous to human life. People associated with organizations such as Operation Rescue and the Environmental Liberation Front, and the World Trade Organization protesters, have engaged in activities that should subject them to prosecution as terrorists."

Furthermore, "once the government decides that conduct is 'domestic terrorism,' law enforcement agents have the authority to charge anyone who provides assistance to that person, even if the assistance is an act as minor as providing lodging. They would have the authority to wiretap the home of anyone who is providing assistance."

"Assistance" includes "support." So, contributions to any group later charged with domestic terrorism—even if the donor was unaware of its range of activities—could lead to an investigation of those giving "support."

As Judge Learned Hand once said, "Liberty lies in the hearts of men and women; when it dies there, no constitution, no law, no court can even do much to help it. While it lies there, it needs no constitution, no law, no court to save it."

We and the Constitution have survived the contempt for the Bill of Rights in the Alien and Sedition Acts of 1798; Abraham Lincoln's suspension of *habeas corpus*, and the jailing of editors and other dissenters during the Civil War; Woodrow Wilson's near annihilation of the First Amendment in the First World War; and the Red Scares of 1919 and the early 1920s when Attorney General A. Mitchell Palmer and his enthusiastic aide, J. Edgar Hoover, rounded up hundreds of "radicals," "subversives," and "Bolsheviks" in thirty-three cities and summarily deported many of them. And we also survived Joe McCarthy. But will liberty still survive "in the hearts" of Americans?

This will be one of our severest tests yet to rescue the Constitution from our government. Benjamin Franklin has been quoted a lot since the USA PATRIOT Act and its progeny. "They that can give up essential liberty to obtain a little temporary safety deserve neither liberty nor safety."

On October 11, 2001, Senator Russ Feingold, dissenting to the PATRIOT Act, said on the floor of the Senate:

> There is no doubt that if we lived in a police state, it would be easier to catch terrorists. If we lived in a country where the police were allowed to search your home at any time for any reason; if we lived in a country where the government is entitled to open your mail, eavesdrop on your phone conversations, or intercept our e-mail communications; if we lived in a country where people

could be held in jail indefinitely based on what they write or think, or based on mere suspicion that they are up to no good, the government would probably discover and arrest more terrorists or would-be terrorists, just as it would find more lawbreakers generally.

But that wouldn't be a country in which we would want to live, and it wouldn't be a country for which we could, in good conscience, ask our young people to fight and die. In short, that country wouldn't be America.

I think it is important to remember that the Constitution was written in 1789 by men who had recently won the Revolutionary War . . . They wrote the Constitution and the Bill of Rights to protect individual liberties in times of war as well as in times of peace.

There have been periods in our nation's history when civil liberties have taken a back seat to what appeared at the time to be legitimate exigencies of war. Our national consciousness still bears the stain and the scars of those events.

We must not allow this piece of our past to become prologue. Preserving our freedom is the reason we are now engaged in this new war on terrorism. We will lose that war without a shot being fired if we sacrifice the liberties of the American people in the belief that by doing so we will stop the terrorists.

Russ Feingold predicted much of what was to come.

CHAPTER THREE

A Society Under Surveillance

> The new [FBI] guidelines emphasize that the FBI must not be deprived of using all lawful authorized methods in investigations, consistent with the Constitution.
>
> —Attorney General John Ashcroft, May 31, 2002

> In reality, Mr. Ashcroft, in the name of fighting terrorism, [is] giving FBI agents nearly unbridled power to poke into the affairs of anyone in the United States, even when there is no evidence of illegal activity.
>
> —Editorial, *New York Times*, May 31, 2002

As usual, television—broadcast and cable—got a key part of the story wrong. The thrust of what they call reporting on the reorganization of the FBI focused on the nine hundred or so new agents, the primacy of intelligence gathering over law enforcement, and the presence of CIA supervisors within the bosom of the FBI. (Remember, it used to be illegal for the CIA to spy on Americans within our borders.)

But the poisonous core of this reorganization is its return to the time of J. Edgar Hoover and COINTELPRO, the counterintelligence operation, pervasively active from 1956 to 1971, that so disgraced the Bureau that it was forced to adopt new guidelines to prevent such wholesale subversion of the Bill of Rights ever again.

Under COINTELPRO, the FBI monitored, infiltrated, manipulated, and secretly fomented divisions within civil rights, antiwar, black, and other entirely lawful organizations that were using the First Amendment to disagree with government policies.

These uninhibited FBI abuses of the Bill of Rights were exposed by some journalists, but most effectively by the Senate Select Committee to Study Governmental Operations with Respect to Intelligence Activities. Its chairman, Frank Church of Idaho, was a true believer in the constitutional guarantees of individual liberties against the government—which is why we had a Revolution.

In 1975, Church told the nation, and J. Edgar Hoover, that COIN-TELPRO had been "a sophisticated vigilante operation aimed squarely at preventing the exercise of First Amendment rights of speech and association." And Church pledged: "The American people need to be reassured that never again will an agency of the government be permitted to conduct a secret war against those citizens it considers a threat to the established order."

Frank Church, however, could not have foreseen George W. Bush, John Ashcroft, and FBI Director Robert Mueller. The guidelines for FBI investigations imposed after COINTELPRO by then Attorney General Edward Levi ordered that agents could not troll for information in churches, libraries, or political meetings of Americans without some leads that someone, somehow, was doing or planning something illegal.

Without even a gesture of consultation with Congress, Ashcroft unilaterally has thrown away those guidelines. From now on, covert FBI agents can mingle with unsuspecting Americans at churches, mosques, synagogues, meetings of environmentalists, the ACLU, the Gun Owners of America, and Reverend Al Sharpton's presidential campaign headquarters. (He has been resoundingly critical of the cutting back of the Bill of Rights.) These eavesdroppers do not need any specific evidence, not even a previous complaint, that anything illegal is going on or is being contemplated.

Laura Murphy, the director of the ACLU's Washington office, puts the danger to us all plainly: "The FBI is now telling the American people, 'You no longer have to do anything unlawful in order to get that knock on the door.'"

During COINTELPRO, I got that knock on the door because I, among other journalists, including some reporters at the *Washington Post*, had been publishing COINTELPRO. More of that FBI visit as we go on.

The attorney general is repeatedly reassuring the American people that there's nothing to worry about. FBI agents, he says, can now go into any public place "under the same terms and conditions as any member of the public."

Really? While the rest of us do not expect privacy in a public place, we also do not expect to be spied upon and put into an FBI dossier because the organizers of the meeting are critical of members of the government, including Ashcroft. We do not expect the casually dressed person next to us to be a secret agent of the attorney general.

Former U.S. Attorney Zachary Carter, best known for his prosecution of the Abner Louima egregious police brutality case, said in the May 31, 2002, *New York Times* that Ashcroft's discarding of the post-COINTELPRO guidelines means that now "law enforcement authorities could conduct investigations that [have] a chilling effect on entirely appropriate lawful expressions of political beliefs, the free exercise of religion, and the freedom of assembly."

So where were the cries of outrage from Democratic leaders Tom Daschle and Dick Gephardt? How do you tell them apart from many Republicans on civil liberties?

Back in 1975, Frank Church issued a warning that is far more pertinent now than it was then. He was speaking of how the government's intelligence capabilities—aimed at "potential" enemies, as well as disloyal Americans—could "at any time" be turned around on the American people, and no American would have any privacy left—such is the capacity to monitor everything, telephone conversations, telegrams, it doesn't matter. There would be no place to hide . . .

"There would be no way to fight back," Church continued, "because the most careful effort to combine together in resistance to the government, no matter how privately it was done, is within the reach of the government to know."

Frank Church could not foresee the extraordinary expansion of electronic surveillance technology, the government's further invasion of the Internet under the new Ashcroft-Mueller guidelines, nor the Magic Lantern that can record every keystroke you make on your computer. But Church's pessimism notwithstanding, there is—and surely will be—more resistance.

The return of COINTELPRO is enshrined in *The Attorney General's Guidelines on General Crimes, Racketeering Enterprise, and Terrorism*

Enterprise Investigations (Department of Justice, May 30, 2002). Since the media have not, by and large, illuminated the actual tripwires in these guidelines, Americans ought to know the perils before them.

On page 3 of the Ashcroft guidelines, we are told: "A terrorism enterprise investigation may be initiated when facts or circumstances reasonably indicate that two or more persons are engaged in an enterprise for the purpose of . . . furthering political or social goals wholly or in part through activities that involve force or violence and a federal crime . . ."

Note the use of "reasonably" and "wholly or in part." These insidiously malleable guidelines for terrorism investigations could apply to political action (and the reaction) during demonstrations by environmentalists, anti-globalizationists, animal rights pickets, or union members on strike, as well as pro-lifers trying to talk, and only to talk, to women entering abortion clinics ("obstruction" at clinics can be a federal crime).

The guidelines go on to note that "*the 'reasonable indication' standard for commencing a terrorism enterprise investigation . . . [is] substantially lower than probable cause.*" It is so low it could be part of the Steven Spielberg–Tom Cruise movie *Minority Report*, which envisions the nabbing of "pre-criminals." As *The Washington Times* puts it, in the movie such "pre-criminals" would be convicted "before they ever act on, or, in some cases, are even aware of their murderous designs." (Emphasis added.)

On page 4 of the Ashcroft guidelines: "The nature of the conduct engaged in by a [terrorist] enterprise will justify an inference that the standard [for opening a criminal intelligence investigation] is satisfied, *even if there are no known statements by participants that advocate or indicate planning for violence or other prohibited acts.*" (Emphasis added.)

The attorney general, furthermore, extends the dragnet to make individuals in a group under suspicion responsible for what other members say or write: "A group's activities and the statements of its members may properly be considered in conjunction with each other. A combination of statements and activities may justify a determination that the threshold standard for a terrorism investigation is satisfied, *even if the statements alone or the activities alone would not warrant such a determination.*" (Emphasis added.)

Also indicating the "pre-crime" mindset of Attorney General Ashcroft is the following paragraph. "While no particular factor or combination of factors is required, considerations that will generally be relevant whether the threshold standard for a terrorism investigation is satisfied includes as noted, a group's statements, its activities, and the nature of *potential* federal law violations *suggested* by its statements or its activities." (Emphasis added)

Keep in mind the massive, pervasive electronic surveillance—with minimal judicial supervision under the USA PATRIOT Act—of inferential "pre-crime" conversations and messages, both sent and received. Add to that the FBI's power, under the same law, to break into your home or office, with a warrant, while you're not there, and insert the Magic Lantern into your computer to record every one of your keystrokes, including those not sent. Then add the PATRIOT Act's allowing the FBI to command bookstores and libraries to reveal the books bought or read by potential domestic terrorists.

In a report on these pervasive invasions of our privacy, the American Civil Liberties Union notes: "It doesn't require some apocalyptic vision of American democracy being replaced by a dictatorship to worry about a surveillance society. There is a lot of room for the United States to become a meaner, less open, and less just place without any radical change in government. All that's required is the continued construction of new surveillance technologies and the simultaneous erosion of privacy protections."

But even the chilling of privacy by continually advancing surveillance technology is less immediate than the realization that, under the Ashcroft FBI guidelines, you are never sure that you are not being covertly watched at a public meeting, in a place of worship, in a library, on the street. As the December 3, 2002, *Wall Street Journal* warned, these Justice Department regulations no longer "require agents to show probable cause that a crime was afoot before spying on political or religious organizations"—or individuals.

As Attorney General Ashcroft pointed out in announcing the new guidelines, FBI agents and other law enforcement personnel are no longer limited by the traditional constitutional privacy safeguards in keeping afoot of where you go and what you say.

Yet, we are continually told by the Bush administration that we are fighting to preserve our freedoms—the American way of life.

CHAPTER FOUR

J. Edgar Hoover Lives!

In the April 1, 1971, *Village Voice* ("Investigating the FBI"), I wrote of having received copies of files on private citizens that had been stolen from the Media, Pennsylvania, office of the FBI. So far as I know, the identities of those who "liberated" these documents have never been discovered by the FBI. There were no names or other clues on the papers I received.

There was, however, a statement of purpose by the people who, earlier that year, had broken into the FBI office. They called themselves the Citizens' Commission to Investigate the FBI and said: "We believe that citizens have the right to scrutinize and control their own government. . . . the FBI has betrayed its democratic trust, and we wish to present evidence for this claim to the open and public judgment of our fellow citizens."

I was not the only recipient of these files in 1971. Although Attorney General John Mitchell, on March 23, urgently asked the press not to publish any of these purloined documents, the next day the *Washington Post* printed a front-page story on the Media, Pennsylvania, operation.

The Washington Post said it was running the substance of the stolen files "in the public interest. . . . We believe the American public . . . needs to think long and hard about whether internal security rests essentially upon official surveillance and the suppression of dissent or upon the traditional freedom of every citizen to speak his mind on any subject, whether others consider what he says wise or foolish, patriotic or subversive."

Having read all the files, and there were many, I wrote in the *Voice* that "none of these people are under surveillance because they have broken any laws." For example, an FBI memorandum said of a college senior under surveillance that she "is known to be an inverterate [sic] Marxist revolutionist, and a type of person that should be watched, as she will probably be very active in revolutionary activities." However, the files also revealed that an FBI informer had talked to this *probably* dangerous young woman "and received no indication that she was anything other than the average liberal-minded student that is common" among those being watched by the FBI. Nonetheless, she was to be kept under surveillance to see whether, in time, she might qualify for insertion into the FBI's Security Index.

The FBI was also very interested in a professor who, along with his wife and children, lived in a "house that numerous college students visit frequently"; the same professor had been inviting "controversial speakers" to his prestigious liberal arts college before "clearing with others." That tip came from the college's chief switchboard operator ("conceal identity due to position at the school").

More than thirty years later, after September 11, 2001, the FBI once again encouraged the citizenry to be watchful—to join the war on terrorism through the Web site of the Internet Fraud Complaint Center (IFCC). As reported in the November 15, 2001, *Washington Post*, the hypertext link near the top of the IFCC's home page (www.ifccfbi.gov) reads: "If you have any information regarding the terrorist attack on September 11, please click here." The TIPS have been streaming in.

On January 8, 2002, the front page of the *Christian Science Monitor* featured a story by Kris Axtman of its Houston bureau: "Political Dissent Can Bring Federal Agents to Door." Her report showed that even though J. Edgar Hoover—whose name graces the FBI building—has departed for the great beyond, the FBI has not lost its zeal.

Indeed, Attorney General John Ashcroft is showing at least as much mettle as Attorney General John Mitchell did when he and Hoover were diligently revising the Constitution. Kris Axtman notes that as the calls mount about various un-Americans, "John Ashcroft's post-September policy is that each tip be looked into."

So it came to pass that, in San Francisco, when sixty-year-old retired phone-company worker Barry Reingold answered the intercom at his residence, two FBI agents announced they were coming up. Earlier, at the gym where Reingold works out, the talk had been about the dread Osama bin Laden, and one of Reingold's fellow gym members had told the FBI about a suspicious turn the conversation had taken.

As Reingold recalled his part of the dialogue at the gym, he had said of the notorious fugitive, "Yeah, he's horrible and did a horrible thing, but Bush has nothing to be proud of. He is a servant of the big oil companies, and his only interest in the Middle East is oil."

After questioning George W. Bush's critic, the FBI agents appeared to clear Reingold of any likely terrorist predilections; but then, after the door closed, Reingold heard one of the agents say, in the corridor, "But we still need to do a report." Mr. Reingold is now a person under suspicion in the FBI's files.

The *Christian Science Monitor* also told of A. J. Brown, a student at Durham Technical Community College in North Carolina. Two Secret Service agents and a Raleigh police officer knocked at her door, telling her they had a tip she had engaged in "un-American activity" in her apartment. Knowing her Constitutional rights, she found out they didn't have a search warrant and refused to let them in. But she answered their questions for forty minutes outside her door.

From the doorway, which was open, her vigilant visitors, as reported by Kris Axtman, saw "a poster of George W. Bush holding a noose. It read: 'We hang on your every word.'" The message was a reminder of Texas Governor Bush's proud record on capital punishment—as the nation's chief executioner. The noose was not around his neck.

Since, under Ashcroft's USA PATRIOT Act, the various intelligence agencies are encouraged to exchange information with one another, I expect A. J. Brown and the noose in her apartment are now in the files of the FBI and the CIA.

Said Barry Steinhardt, associate director of the American Civil Liberties Union: "It's a very frightening trend: that people are doing nothing more than expressing the very freedoms we are fighting to preserve and find themselves with the FBI at the door.

CHAPTER FIVE

The FBI Eyeing What You Read

The December 25, 2001, issue of *Capital Times*, a newspaper in Madison, Wisconsin, ran a warning about how the FBI, under Attorney General John Ashcroft and the USA PATRIOT Act, can order bookstores to provide lists of books bought by people suspected of involvement in terrorism.

The definition of terrorism in the USA PATRIOT Act is so broad and vague that any number of American readers may be caught in this additional Ashcroft dragnet. For example, you commit "the crime of domestic terrorism if [any of your acts] appear to be intended to . . . influence the policy of a government by intimidation." Such "acts" could be based on what you read in a book.

From the *Capital Times*: "At A Room of One's Own [bookstore] . . . which stocks women's literature and women's studies texts but also gay and lesbian erotica, owner Sandy Torkildson does not keep sales records by purchaser name, in order to protect her customers. 'I think this law is a real threat,' she said."

This threat was described in a November 1, 2002, letter to booksellers across the country by Chris Finan, president of the American Booksellers Foundation for Free Expression. Finan's letter and his fears for the First Amendment received hardly any mention in the press aside from the *Capital Times* and *The Progressive* magazine.

"[Under Section 215 of the USA PATRIOT Act] the director of the FBI may seek an order 'for any tangible things (including books, records, papers, documents, and other items) for an investigation to protect against international terrorism or clandestine activities.'

"The request for such an order is to be made to a judge who sits in a special court that is sometimes called the 'spy court.'" This is the secret court established by the Foreign Intelligence Surveillance Act (FISA) in 1978. On its bench sit federal judges selected by the

Chief Justice of the Supreme Court; they receive requests for subpoenas and warrants from federal agents engaged in investigating terrorism.

Chris Finan's letter to the country's booksellers continued: "The judge makes his decision *ex parte*, meaning there is no opportunity for you or your lawyer to object in court. *You cannot object publicly, either. The new law includes a gag order that prevents you from disclosing 'to any other person' the fact that you have received an order to produce documents.*" (Emphasis added.)

And this is the United States of America, John Ashcroft, Attorney General—not the People's Republic of China?

Chris Finan goes on: "American Booksellers for Free Expression is deeply concerned by the potential chilling effect of court orders issued to booksellers under this new law. Normally, when a bookseller receives a [court order] for customer information, he or she has the opportunity to ask the court to quash the order on First Amendment grounds. In several cases, booksellers have successfully resisted subpoenas. Under FISA, however, booksellers may not have this chance. Depending on the wording of the order, the bookseller may be required to *immediately* turn over the records that are being sought." (Emphasis added.)

This is yet another moment in Ashcroft-Bush time when George Orwell should still be with us. This command to turn over the names of book buyers—and borrowers of library books—has a deceptive exception, as noted in the USA PATRIOT Act. "Such investigation [as demanding library records] of a United States person is not conducted solely upon the basis of activities protected by the First Amendment to the Constitution."

The freedom to read is not already protected by the First Amendment? Well, the semanticists at the Department of Justice have interpreted that phrase to mean that you—"a United States person"—are still protected by the First Amendment if you stand on a corner and make a speech.

But if the FBI has a suspicion that you may be connected to international terrorism or clandestine intelligence activities, they can find out what you're reading, despite the First Amendment. A Thomas Paine book advocating revolution, for instance?

So what can a bookseller do when the FBI comes calling? Chris Finan tells bookstore owners:

> You remain entitled to legal counsel. Therefore, you may call your attorney and/or the American Booksellers Foundation for Free Expression. Because of the gag order, however, you should not tell us that you have received a court order under the Foreign Intelligence Surveillance Act. You can simply tell us that you need to contact [our] legal counsel. . . .
>
> It may be possible for you to have a lawyer present during a search of your store records. If so, the lawyer will be able to help you ensure that there is no violation of the privacy of your other customers. However, it is possible that the FBI will demand immediate access to your records.
>
> If the agents are unwilling to permit you to contact your attorney, you should cooperate with them. *Otherwise, you may be arrested for disobeying a court order. If you have no choice but to turn over your records, the best thing you can do is help the FBI find the information that it is looking for and thus avoid exposing the records of other customers.* (Emphasis added).

That is, if you can swiftly remove information about presumably "innocent" customers quickly enough.

The *Capital Times* in Madison, Wisconsin, quotes Barbara Dimick, director of the Madison Public Library. She says: "We want to be able to tell people who use the library that records are confidential, and they can use materials without fear of intimidation. That's being usurped now by federal agents. . . . We're all real jittery about it."

Adding to the unease among librarians around the country was the Draconian gag order. Courts do infrequently impose gag orders preceding or during trials, and the media often successfully fight to overturn them. But never in the history of the First Amendment has any suppression of speech by the government been so sweeping and difficult to contest as this one by Ashcroft.

For example, if a judge places a gag order on the press in a case before the court, the press can at least print the fact that it's been silenced, and the public will know about it. But now, under this provision of the USA PATRIOT Act, how does the press track what's going on? How many bookstores and libraries will have their records seized? Are any of them bookstores or libraries that you frequent? Are these court orders part of FBI fishing expeditions, like Ashcroft's mass roundups of immigrants?

And if the FBI deepens its concerns about terrorist leanings after inspecting a suspect's reading list, how can everyone else know what books will make the FBI worry about us?

As one First Amendment lawyer said to me, "What makes this so chilling is that there is no input into the process." First there is the secrecy in which the subpoenas are obtained—with only the FBI present in court. Then there is the gag order commanding the persons receiving the subpoenas to remain silent.

Has John Ashcroft been reading Franz Kafka lately?

Only by getting more and more Americans to realize that they themselves—not just noncitizens—can be affected by these amputations of the Bill of Rights will there be a critical mass of resistance to what Ashcroft and Bush are doing to our liberties. Accordingly, the press must awaken the citizenry not only to the FBI's harvesting lists of what "suspect" Americans read, but also to the judicial silencing of bookstores and libraries that are being compelled to betray the privacy and First Amendment rights of readers.

George Orwell said: "If large numbers of people believe in freedom of speech, there will be freedom of speech even if the law forbids it. But if public opinion is sluggish, inconvenient minorities will be persecuted, even if laws exist to protect them."

CHAPTER SIX

Burglars with Badges

Others say, Law is our Fate;
Others say, Law is our State;
Others say, others say
Law is no more,
Law has gone away.

—W. H. Auden

There were some members of Congress who feared—as the Bush-Ashcroft antiterrorism bill was rushed through—that the Constitution was in the line of fire. But as the lead editorial in the October 26, 2001, *Washington Post* ("A Panicky Bill") noted: "Members with reservations feared objecting lest there be a further terrorist attack and they be blamed for having failed to give the government the means to prevent it."

Then, when a "sunset" clause was agreed to—requiring Congress to review its handiwork in four years—uneasy members figured they could repair any holes in the Bill of Rights at that time. But if the terrorists—including the "sleepers" hidden among us—are not obliterated in four years, well, the citizenry will want to give up even more of its freedoms. And Congress will not dare stand in the way.

However, one of the worst assaults on our liberties in the USA PATRIOT Act is *not* subject to the sunset clause. It is now a permanent part of our laws. The new act includes "Sneak and Peek Warrants," as they are cosmetically called now. In J. Edgar Hoover's day, they were known as warrantless "black bag jobs." Ashcroft legalizes, with warrants, burglars with FBI badges.

As described by the American Civil Liberties Union, this provision "would allow law enforcement agencies to delay giving notice when they conduct a search. This means that the government could enter a house, apartment, or office with a search warrant when the occupant was away, search through her property and take photographs, and in some cases, seize physical property and electronic communications, and not tell her until later. This provision would mark a sea change in the way search warrants are executed in the United States."

What is particularly ominous about these secret searches is underlined by Boston University law professor Tracey Maclin, a leading expert on the Fourth Amendment. In the November 5, 2001, *National Law Journal*, Maclin warned that these break-ins are "not tied [only] to cases in which national security or threats from foreign agents appear to be the focus of investigations. *It can apply to any intrusion.*" (Emphasis added.) That is, any criminal investigation.

Rule 41 (d) of the Federal Rules of Criminal Procedure specifically requires that the officer conducting the search shall "leave a copy and receipt at the place from which the property was taken."

With timely notice of a black bag job, you can challenge it in court before any action is taken against you. Did the FBI go to the wrong address? Did the official burglars take only what the warrant allowed them to take? And if you know what they did take, you will be able to justify your noncriminal possession of what is now in their hands.

Previously, there has been limited authority to delay notice of a secret search—if, the ACLU notes, "an individual's physical safety will be endangered, someone will flee prosecution, evidence will be tampered with, potential witnesses will be intimidated, or an investigation will be jeopardized or a trial unduly delayed."

But now, the ACLU continues, Section 213 of the USA PATRIOT Act would take this limited authority "and expand it so that it will be available in any kind of search (physical or electronic) and in any kind of criminal case. . . . Law enforcement agents will seek to delay notification whenever it is to their advantage to do so. Over time, the delayed notice 'exception' would become the rule and would deal another serious blow to the privacy protections afforded by the Fourth Amendment."

As soon as the antiterrorism bill was signed by the president, Attorney General Ashcroft instructed all the United States attorneys and the FBI to push the provisions of this new law to the limit. That includes break-ins.

Section 213 of the new law does say that notice of a secret search is to be given within "a reasonable period." Ashcroft's Justice Department interprets that to mean within ninety days. But the government can ask a judge to extend that period for "good cause." As Rachel King, legislative counsel for the ACLU in Washington, tells me, extensions can be granted indefinitely. Remember that these black bag jobs—where no one leaves a receipt for what has been taken—apply to *any* criminal investigation, not only to terrorism probes.

Professor Maclin makes the necessary point: "It's all a question of how we view the Fourth Amendment. The amendment's essential purpose is to control the discretion of government officials to intrude in our lives. How many judges, particularly where criminal contraband is discovered, are going to say the government's request is unreasonable? They're not going to do it." And, if the government claims that the criminal investigation is also based on a suspicion of terrorist activity, what judge will refuse as many delays of notice as the FBI, or any other agency, ardently desires?

Supreme Court Justice William Brennan once told me his belief that the key precipitating cause of the American Revolution was the "general writ of assistance" that allowed the British to search and seize whatever they wanted in the colonists' homes and businesses.

As I've noted, the Committees of Correspondence spread the word of these infuriating abuses of privacy throughout the colonies, as in this report from Boston: "Our houses and even our bed chambers are exposed to be ransacked, our boxes, chests, and trunks broke open, ravaged, and plundered. . . . Flagrant instances of the wanton exercise of this power have frequently happened. . . . By this we are cut off from that domestic security which renders the lives of the most unhappy in some measure agreeable."

In 1761, James Otis challenged a new British writ of assistance in the Massachusetts Superior Court: "A man's house is his castle. . . . This writ, if it should be declared legal, would totally annihilate this privilege." It was declared legal, and the Declaration of Independence was a result.

And that's why we have a Fourth Amendment, to prevent such abuses from happening ever again. Or rather, we *had* a Fourth Amendment, which says:

> The right of the people to be secure in their persons, houses, papers, and effects, against unreasonable searches and seizures, shall not be violated, and no Warrants shall issue, but upon probable cause, supported by Oath or affirmation, and particularly describing the place to be searched, and the persons or things to be seized. (Ratified December 1791.)

CHAPTER SEVEN

The FBI's Magic Lantern

Before being confirmed for the Supreme Court, Louis Brandeis was known as the People's Lawyer because he was pro-labor and fought monopolies and trusts. It took months before the Senate agreed to put this "Radical" on the court as the first Jew in its history. Brandeis was particularly passionate about the right to privacy, and one of his dissents on that issue foresaw the Bush-Ashcroft administration's ominous assaults on that right.

In 1928, the first wiretapping case, *Olmstead v. U.S.*, came before the Court. A majority of Brandeis's brethren ruled that wiretapping a phone without a warrant did not violate the Fourth and Fifth Amendments because the taps were planted *outside* the home.

Brandeis, who was widely read and suspicious of government's overreaching tentacles, wrote prophetically that "in the application of a Constitution, our contemplation cannot be only of what has been, but of what may be. The progress of science in furnishing the government with means of espionage is not likely to stop with wiretapping. Ways may some day be developed by which the government, without removing papers from secret drawers, can reproduce them in court, and by which it will be enabled to expose to a jury the most intimate occurrences of the home. . . . Can it be that the Constitution affords no protection against such invasions of individual security?"

Brandeis could not anticipate the advent of the computer and the Internet, but his prophecy, as I've noted, has come true. Already, as Reuters reported on December 12, 2001, the FBI has asked "Internet service providers to install technology in their networks that allows officials to secretly read e-mails of criminal investigation targets." That molestation of privacy was called "Carnivore." But the FBI has developed an even more insidious device to obtain "the most intimate occurrences of the home"—and office.

Beware of the "Magic Lantern." Under the "sneak and peek" provision of the USA PATRIOT Act, pushed through Congress by John Ashcroft, the FBI, with a warrant, can break into your home and office when you're not there and, on the first trip, look around. As I pointed out previously, they can examine your hard drive, snatch files, and plant the Magic Lantern on your computer. It's also known as the "sniffer keystroke logger." Jim Dempsey, deputy director of the Washington-based Center for Democracy and Technology, tells me that you have to be remarkably computer-savvy to detect the presence of the Magic Lantern in some crevice in your computer.

Once installed, the Magic Lantern creates a record of every time you press a key on the computer. It's all saved in plain text, and during the FBI's next secret visit to your home or office, that information is downloaded as the agents also pick up whatever other records and papers they find of interest. These legal break-ins, including the use of the Magic Lantern, are not limited to investigations of terrorism but are now part of regular criminal investigations.

By the way, in case you might be just musing at the computer—typing in thoughts or theories you don't intend to send—the Magic Lantern will capture those strokes, too.

And, Jim Dempsey notes, if they don't find anything the first and second times, they can keep breaking into your home or office until they come across a smoking gun. Eventually, they'll have to tell you they've been there.

But Justice Brandeis predicted that the government one day would be able to remove private materials *without* physically having to go into hour home or office. Well, never underestimate the capacity of advancing technology to further diminish what little is left of your privacy.

Reuters also has reported that the Magic Lantern would allow "the agency [the FBI] to plant a Trojan horse keystroke logger on a target's PC by sending a computer virus over the Internet, rather than require physical access to the computer as is now the case."

The Reuters December 12, 2001, story quotes the FBI as claiming the Magic Lantern itself "is a workbench project" that has not yet been deployed. But I have a copy of a May 8, 1999, application to a

United States District Court in New Jersey from a U.S. Attorney in that state at the time, Faith Hochberg. It authorizes a "surreptitious entry" to search and seize "encryption key related pass phrases from [a] computer by installing a specialized computer program ... which will allow the Government to read and interpret data that was previously seized pursuant to a search warrant."

The application also asks permission for the FBI or its delegated entities to enter the location "surreptitiously, covertly, and by breaking and entering, if necessary"—and "as many times as may be necessary to install, maintain, and remove the software, firmware, or hardware."

CHAPTER EIGHT

Computers Will Say
Who We Are

How often, or on what system, the Thought Police plugged in
any individual wire was guesswork. It was even conceivable that
they watched everybody all the time. But at any rate, they could
plug in your wire whenever they wanted to.

—George Orwell, *1984*

The writers who most influenced me were Charles Dickens (a superb
journalist—in his appalled description of a hanging at New York's
Tombs, for example—as well as an enduring novelist) and Arthur
Koestler (whose *Darkness at Noon* taught me when I was fifteen that
dishonest means irredeemably corrupt all ends, no matter how
noble). But above all was George Orwell, who, like Henry David
Thoreau, listened to his own drum.

Orwell died in 1950. Prophetic as he was in 1984, however, he could
not have imagined how advanced surveillance technology would
become. His novel is now being actualized in real time at the Defense
Department, headed by the Washington press corps's favorite cabinet officer, the witty Donald Rumsfeld.

John Markoff of the *New York Times* broke this story on February
13, 2002, when he wrote that retired Admiral John Poindexter,
national security adviser for President Ronald Reagan, "has returned
to the Pentagon to direct a new agency that is developing technologies to give federal officials access to vast new surveillance and
information-analysis systems."

There was scarcely any follow-up in the media until Markoff, on
November 9, aroused the dozing press by reporting that "the Pentagon
is constructing a computer system that could create a vast electronic
dragnet, searching for personal information as part of the hunt for ter-

rorists around the globe—including the United States." At first the Defense Department, without any official public notice, and without any congressional hearings—with an initial appropriation of $200 million—was constructing the Terrorism Information Awareness System (originally the Total Information Awareness System).

It will extensively mine government and commercial data banks, enabling the FBI, the CIA, and other intelligence agencies to collect information that will allow the government—as noted on ABC-TV's November 14, 2002, *Nightline*—"to essentially reconstruct the movements of citizens." This will be done without warrants from courts, thereby making individual privacy as obsolete as the sauropods of the Mesozoic era. (Intelligence data from, and to, foreign sources will also be involved.)

Our government's unblinking eyes will try to find suspicious patterns in your credit card and bank data, medical records, the movies you click for on pay-per-view, passport applications, prescription purchases, e-mail messages, telephone calls, and anything you've done that winds up in court records, such as divorces. Almost anything you do will leave a trace for these omnivorous computers, which will now contain records of your library book withdrawals, your loans and debts, and whatever you order by mail or on the Web.

As Georgetown University law professor Jonathan Turley pointed out in the November 17 *Los Angeles Times*, "For more than two hundred years, our liberties have been protected primarily by practical barriers—rather than constitutional barriers—to government abuse. Because of the sheer size of the nation and its population, the government could not practically abuse a great number of citizens at any given time. In the last decade, however, these practical barriers have fallen to technology."

Once the story of Americans being under constant surveillance began to have legs, press interest was particularly heightened by the Defense Department's choice to head this unintended tribute to George Orwell. Poindexter, as Turley reminded us, "was the master architect behind the Iran-Contra scandal, the criminal conspiracy to sell arms to a terrorist nation, Iran, in order to surreptitiously fund an unlawful clandestine project in Nicaragua."

Poindexter was convicted of lying to Congress and destroying documents. His sentence was reversed because he had been granted immunity for testifying in the case. But the evidence against him stands. So this lawbreaker has been put in charge of a project, paid for by our tax dollars, to direct all kinds of personal information on all of us into interconnected computers.

As Richard Cohen wrote in the *Washington Post*, ("Watched and Listed," November 21, 2002), "Soon, another computer—this one a behemoth—will reassemble us digitally, authoritatively, and we will be what it says we are." In all the media stories I've seen on this creation of a real-life Big Brother, Poindexter's boss, Donald Rumsfeld, has gotten a pass from the press in that he escapes mention as the Bush cabinet member who approved the hiring of Poindexter. And since Rumsfeld is a hands-on administrator, he must surely know what Poindexter is doing with his initial $200 million budget.

As usual, George W. Bush, the commander in chief of the Pentagon, has been ignored by the press as the ultimate authorizer of the Terrorism Information Awareness System—except for one reference. Queried about Poindexter's Iran-Contra history, Bush said, "Admiral Poindexter has served our nation very well."

In Orwell's 1984, "the telescreen [at home] received and transmitted simultaneously," so that the viewer could be seen and heard by Big Brother. Now under development are advanced forms of interactive television that will also make this Orwell prophecy real.

Meanwhile, on National Public Radio, Larry Abramson reported that the Office of Information Awareness, which Poindexter heads, is developing techniques of "face recognition, using CCTV camera systems that would allow government officials to identify individuals moving in public space." As we move, we could also be identified by the way we walk or the sound of our voices. And in an editorial, the *Washington Post* (November 16, 2002) added, "If computers can learn to identify a person through a video camera, then constant surveillance of society becomes possible too." Paul Werbos, an artificial intelligence specialist at the National Science Foundation and a computer expert, asks: "How many innocent people are going to be falsely included. How many terrorists are going to slip through?"

The United States Senate—which seldom rises against the administration's reductions of the Bill of Rights—unanimously passed an amendment, however, in January 2003, to an omnibus spending bill, that suspended the deployment and continued development of the Terrorism Information Awareness system until there is extensive consultation with Congress.

The administration, taken aback, proposed a compromise. It pledged to assure Congress of increased privacy protections in the omnivorous data-mining project by setting up both an external watchdog advisory committee of prominent citizens and an internal Defense Department board of senior civilian officials. This was to calm the fears of Congress and the public that George Orwell's 1984 has indeed been created by the government—in real time.

But any compromise with such a pervasive continuing, constant accumulation of personal data on just about all Americans—in government and private data banks—is fanciful. Once this fearsome technology is in place—to be shared by all government intelligence and law-enforcement agencies—there would be only an illusion of privacy protections.

Unless, of course, you trust the government, any administration, to be scrupulously circumspect in limiting its net of persons under suspicion while taking great pains to ensure that all the massive data pouring in is accurate—including the multiple associations of the persons under suspicion, some of which might include you.

Despite the suspension by the Senate of the Terrorism Information Awareness System, Admiral Poindexter continues to expand its technological capacities.

CHAPTER NINE

The Patriot Enforcers

In 1950, Republican Senator Margaret Chase Smith of Maine was the first member of Congress to publicly confront Senator Joseph McCarthy's charges that those who disagreed with his version of patriotism were—as Attorney General John Ashcroft now says of his critics—giving "ammunition to America's enemies."

At the time, Margaret Chase Smith was the only woman in the Senate. She led six other senators in presenting a Declaration of Conscience to the rest of her colleagues—urging them to protect individual liberties from the likes of McCarthy. It took four more years for the Senate to censure Joe McCarthy.

What Senator Smith said on that day ought to be studied not only by the president and the attorney general of the United States but also by certain editorial writers at the New York *Daily News* and the *New York Post* who have attacked members of the city's Community School District 3 for defying the Board of Education's edict that the Pledge of Allegiance must be recited daily in every classroom in our public schools.

"Those of us who shout the loudest about Americanism," Margaret Chase Smith said, "are all too frequently those who . . . ignore some of the basic principles of Americanism—the right to criticize, the right to hold unpopular beliefs, the right to protest, the right of independent thought."

Are there any teachers in the nation's school systems who would dare defy John Ashcroft and tell their students about Margaret Chase Smith and her Declaration of Conscience, and how it applies to what's going on now?

Many enforcers of patriotism on school boards throughout the country have also been commanding after 9/11 that the Pledge of Allegiance be intoned every day. In some cities and towns, as in New York, students are actually informed that they can refuse to stand and pledge as an act of conscience—by order of the Supreme Court of the United states in 1943 (*West Virginia State Board of Education v. Barnette*).

But a student who remains seated or is sent to the principal's office so as not to disturb the ritual is often treated as a pariah by his or her fellow students. For one of many examples, some years ago, a brave young woman in a California high school was pursued down the corridors repeatedly by enraged student patriots of whom John Ashcroft would be proud. Other dissenters, defended by the ACLU, have had to go to the courts, which have reprimanded boards of education and principals for ignoring the rudiments of the First Amendment.

In New York, editorial writers at the *Daily News* and the *New York Post* directed their fire, with particular outrage, at Larry Sauer, a District 3 school board member who made the motion to have each of the schools in the district decide how to deal with the Pledge of Allegiance rather than mandating them all to fall in line. Said Sauer, "Requiring students to blindly repeat the pledge is no different than the [then] Taliban requiring children to memorize the Koran and repeat it by rote, without understanding why or what they are saying." A more cogent analogy would have been to one of our current allies in the war on terrorism—the People's Republic of China, which routinely jails political prisoners of conscience.

The *New York Post*, noting that District 3 covers the Upper West Side, characteristically added that this section of the city was "once termed, for good reason, 'Moscow-on-the-Hudson.' Condemning America is par for the course in much of that left-wing loony bin." In its invincible ignorance, the *Post* does not realize that in this comment it is jubilantly engaging in McCarthyism.

And the *Daily News* charged that District 3 "is afraid that patriotism may not be suitable for children. That sound you hear is Osama bin Laden laughing."

Years ago, I pledged that once every year I would print part of the clearest and most fundamental definition of Americanism in our history so far—Supreme Court Justice Robert Jackson's majority opinion in the aforementioned *West Virginia State Board of Education v. Barnette.* I haven't always kept my word. However, I can't think of a better time to recall this testament of why we are Americans.

Because saluting the flag violated their religious beliefs, the children of Jehovah's Witnesses refused to participate in the mandatory Pledge of Allegiance in the West Virginia public schools. They were expelled and then threatened, as Justice Jackson noted, with being "sent to reformatories maintained for criminally inclined juveniles. In West Virginia, parents of such children have been prosecuted . . . for causing delinquency." To a Jehovah's Witness, saluting the flag is bowing down to a "graven image," which is forbidden in Exodus 20:4–5.

In his decision, Jackson, while affirming the free-exercise-of-religion clause of the First Amendment, emphasized the corollary rights of freedom of conscience and belief for all Americans, religious or not:

> That [boards of education] are educating the young for citizenship is reason for scrupulous protection of constitutional freedoms of the individual, if we are not to strangle the free mind at its source and teach youth to discount important principles of our government as mere platitudes. . . .
>
> Freedom to differ is not limited to things that do not matter much. That would be a mere shadow of freedom. The test of its substance is the right to differ as to things that touch the heart of the existing order.

Jackson's opinion then thundered:

> *If there is any fixed star in our constellation, it is that no official, high or petty, can prescribe what shall be orthodox in politics, nationalism, religion, or other matters of opinion, or force citizens to confess by word or act their faith therein.* (Emphasis added.)

He concluded:

> We think the action of the local authorities in compelling the flag salute and pledge transcends constitutional lim-

itations on their power and invades the sphere of intellect and spirit which it is the purpose of the First Amendment to our Constitution to reserve from all official control.

The Jehovah's Witness children returned to school and did not have to stand and pledge to the flag. This Supreme Court decision was handed down during our war against Hitler.

John Ashcroft scorns his critics for scaring Americans "with phantoms of lost liberty." What actually scares more and more of us is his and the president's dangerous ignorance of the essence of Americanism.

CHAPTER TEN

A Citizen Shorn of All Rights

The government has taken the position that with no meaningful judicial review, an American citizen alleged to be an enemy
combatant could be detained indefinitely without charges or
counsel on the government's say-so.

–American Bar Association Task Force on Treatment of Enemy
Combatants, Preliminary Report, August 8, 2002

The accumulation of all powers, legislative, executive, and judiciary, in the same hands . . . may justly be pronounced the very
definition of tyranny.

–James Madison, *Federalist Papers*, 47

Yaser Esam Hamdi's name has become familiar and troubling to
constitutional lawyers, but it has little resonance yet to Americans at
large. However, what happens to him in our system of justice will signal how far the courts—eventually the Supreme Court—will allow
George W. Bush, John Ashcroft, and Donald Rumsfeld to create what
Charles Lane, the *Washington Post*'s Supreme Court reporter, accurately calls "a parallel legal system in which terrorism suspects—U.S.
citizens and noncitizens alike—may be investigated, jailed, interro-
gated, held, and punished without legal protections guaranteed by the
ordinary system."

If unchecked by the courts—and Congress—Bush's parallel legal
system will push the Constitution aside and realize James Madison's
prediction that when all power is commanded by only one of the
three branches of government, those ensnared in that rogue system
are powerless.

Yaser Esam Hamdi, born in Louisiana of Saudi parents, was captured by Northern Alliance forces in Afghanistan. He was transferred
to Camp X-Ray in the Guantánamo Naval Base in Cuba. When his

American captors realized Hamdi is an American citizen, he was taken, in April 2002, to a naval station brig in Norfolk, Virginia, where he has since been held without any charges or trial, without access to his public defender, and without being able to see his family or anyone else. This American citizen, incommunicado and stripped of his constitutional rights, has been put in this condition by direct order of the president of the United States.

On October 24, 2002, the New York–based Center for Constitutional Rights, Human Rights Watch, and eighteen other human rights groups, plus a coalition of 139 law professors, submitted an *amicus* brief to the Fourth Circuit Court of Appeals charging that "the detention of American citizen Yaser Esam Hamdi is unconstitutional."

Reading the brief, keep in mind that the Bush administration has plans to set up "enemy combatant" detention facilities for other American citizens (*Wall Street Journal*, August 8, 2002).

In stark language, the brief goes on to say that "the government's position is that the president has complete discretion to suspend the application of the Bill of Rights and the writ of *habeas corpus* [which requires the government to prove the legality of a person's imprisonment] to American citizens on American soil, without the authority of Congress or the courts." The Bush administration has stated this position in *Hamdi v. Rumsfeld* (Fourth Circuit, July 12, 2002). The government also maintains that this American citizen, Hamdi, can be held indefinitely.

Accordingly, the Center for Constitutional Rights' *amicus* brief continues: "We urge this court to declare, now and for future generations, that American citizens have a right not to be detained indefinitely, without due process, and that substantive judicial review is indispensable to the Constitution's guarantee of these rights."

It is not mere rhetoric to point out that the future of the Constitution for generations to come is at stake.

Hamdi has had a court hearing, although he himself was not allowed to be present. The judge in the Federal District Court in Norfolk, Virginia, is Robert Doumar, a Reagan appointee, who is passionate about assuring due process—fairness under the Constitution—to all who appear before him. In that admirable sense, he is a "strict constructionist."

In open court, this seventy-two-year-old jurist, who insists on ensuring the separation of powers in the governance of this nation, said: "This case appears to be the first in American jurisprudence where an American citizen has been held incommunicado and subjected to an indefinite detention in the continental United States without charges . . . and without access to a lawyer." (A George Bush contribution to American history!) Hamdi, in his windowless room in the floating navy brig, has yet to meet his lawyer, Frank Dunham Jr.

Judge Doumar demanded the government's explanation of its basis in law for imprisoning Hamdi in that brig. Gregory G. Garre, an assistant to Solicitor General Theodore Olson—who is a major player in the Bush administration's rewiring of the Constitution—handed the judge an official sworn document, only two pages long, by Michael Mobbs, a special adviser to the undersecretary of defense for policy.

In "Meet Mr. Mobbs" (www.usnews.com, October 21, 2002), Angie Cannon describes Mobbs as "wired into a network of politically influential conservatives going back to his days as an arms control negotiator in the Reagan administration." She adds that while a student at Yale, Mobbs "played in the jazz orchestra." Nonetheless, the spirit of freedom embodied in the canon of Louis Armstrong and other jazz masters has eluded Mr. Mobbs.

As *The Economist*, London, said on December 14, 2002:

> It is hard to imagine that America would look kindly on a foreign government that demanded the right to hold some of its own citizens in prison, incommunicado, denying them access to legal assistance for as long as it thought necessary, without ever charging them with a crime.

Nevertheless, that is the position that George Bush's administration has tried to defend in the courts with regard to American citizens whom it has deemed to be "enemy combatants."

Before getting to the judge's angry reaction to the Mobbs statement, it's necessary to note that just about every reference to Hamdi in the media has said—as printed in the November 1, 2002, *New York Law Journal*—that "Hamdi was seized while fighting with the Taliban in Afghanistan." How do we know that to be true? Don't you trust your source—your government?

As Katherine Seelye wrote in the *New York Times* (August 13, 2002) of Judge Doumar's response to the official Mobbs document giving the government's evidence: "He made very clear that he found the statement lacking in nearly every respect."

A fuller account of what Judge Doumar said is in an extraordinarily valuable report by the Lawyers Committee for Human Rights: *A Year of Loss: Reexamining Civil Liberties Since September 11*. Released September 5, 2002, the report quotes more of what Judge Doumar indignantly said to the government prosecutor who had handed him the Mobbs document: "I'm challenging everything in the Mobbs declaration. If you think I don't understand the utilization of words, you are sadly mistaken."

Mr. Mobbs had declared that Hamdi was "affiliated with a Taliban unit and received weapons training." Bolstering the government's case—or so it seemed—were photographs in some of the media of Hamdi carrying a weapon. So what was Judge Doumar's beef?

The Mobbs document, Judge Doumar said bluntly, "makes no effort to explain what 'affiliated' means nor under what criteria this 'affiliation' justified Hamdi's classification as an enemy combatant.

> The declaration is silent as to what level of 'affiliation' is necessary to warrant enemy combatant status. ... It does not say where or by whom he received weapons training or the nature and content thereof.
>
> Indeed, a close inspection of the declaration reveals that [it] *never claims that Hamdi was fighting for the Taliban, nor that he was a member of the Taliban*. ... Without access to the screening criteria actually used by the government in its classification decision, this Court is unable to determine whether the government has paid adequate consideration to due process rights to which Hamdi is entitled under his present detention. (Emphasis added)

Think about that. This American citizen was officially stripped of all his constitutional rights and this flimsy two-page document is the government's explanation before the court. If the government had more information, why didn't it show that evidence *in camera* (to the judge in his private chambers)?

I doubt that the relatively few Americans—not counting constitutional lawyers—who have been following this crucial case know how thoroughly Judge Doumar discredited the government's explanation for its indefinite punishment—without charges—of Hamdi.

Another point, this one entirely ignored by the media, is in an *amicus* brief to the Fourth Court of Appeals by the National Association of Criminal Defense Lawyers:

> [The government claims] that Mr. Hamdi "surrendered" not to U.S. forces, but to a group of counter-insurgent Afghanis popularly called the "Northern Alliance." However, [the government then proceeds] to repeatedly claim that Hamdi was "captured"—an important distinction when evaluating his legal status *vis-à-vis* the United States and under international law. One who surrenders *before* engaging in "combat" can hardly be classified as a "combatant" logically, much less legally.

In addition to Mr. Mobbs's pieces of paper, the government prosecutor also told Judge Doumar that the Defense Department had to hold Hamdi for interrogation. And since the war on terrorism has no defined end in sight, he must be "detained" indefinitely.

Said Judge Doumar: "How long does it take to question a man? A year? Two years? Ten years? A lifetime? How long?"

Under this intensive fire, the prosecutor, Gregory G. Garre, an assistant to Solicitor General Theodore Olson, had only this response: "The present detention is lawful."

As Judge Doumar said after he had denounced the two-page declaration: "So the Constitution doesn't apply to Mr. Hamdi?"

CHAPTER ELEVEN

Liberty's Court of Last Resort

Mr. Hamdi could, in fact, be entirely innocent, and yet the court says there is no judicial recourse.

—Georgetown University law professor David Cole, National Public Radio, January 8, 2003

During one of our last conversations, the late Supreme Court Justice William Brennan said, "Look, pal, we've always known—the Framers knew—that liberty is a fragile thing."

Liberty has become much more fragile under the Bush-Ashcroft-Rumsfeld administration. On December 8, 2002, the Fourth Circuit Court of Appeals handed Bush's team its most significant victory so far in inflicting collateral damage on the Bill of Rights in the war on terrorism.

A unanimous three-judge panel ruled that twenty-two-year-old Yaser Esam Hamdi, an American citizen, can be imprisoned indefinitely in a navy brig on American soil.

Conceivably, Hamdi, if the government continues not to charge him with any crime, will be released only when the open-ended war on terrorism is over, if he lives that long. The president, on his sole authority, put Hamdi in that prison. And unless Hamdi's court of last resort, the Supreme Court, restores his basic constitutional rights as an American citizen, he will stay behind bars. There will be an appeal to the Supreme Court.

The Fourth Circuit's ruling has been hailed by John Ashcroft as "an important victory for the president's ability to protect the American people in times of war."

But, in view of the thinness of the government's case against Hamdi, as the lower court judge emphasized, consider this peculiar reasoning in the Fourth Circuit's decision:

The factual averments in the affidavit, *if accurate*, are sufficient to confirm that Hamdi's detention conforms with a legitimate exercise of the war powers given to the executive. . . . Asking the executive [the president] to provide more detailed factual assertions would be to wade further into the conduct of war than we consider appropriate and is unnecessary to a meaningful judicial review of this question. (Emphasis added)

According to the Bush administration, an American citizen can be held indefinitely, incommunicado, on its say-so that the government's facts are actually factual. This is due process? This is America? Yet the Fourth Circuit stated in the same decision that stripping any citizen of his or her constitutional protections "is not a step that any court would casually take."

Hamdi has not been allowed to be interviewed by his lawyer so that the government can be cross-examined in court on the credibility of its affidavit. In the January 9, 2003, *Washington Post*, Stephen Dycus, an expert in national security law at the Vermont Law School, said plainly and irrefutably that Hamdi is "not being given the right to refute the charges against him."

Dycus also made the crucial point that "despite some lip service about the courts preserving some role for themselves [in this case], the [Fourth Circuit] really doesn't play that role." And, as Dycus emphasized, it is the president who has "the last word" on whether the evidence against Hamdi is to be believed. Trust Bush. He's the commander in chief. But the Constitution explicitly insists on the separation of powers. That's why we have the judiciary.

Keep in mind what Judge Doumar said: "A close inspection of the declaration reveals that [it] *never claims that Hamdi was fighting for the Taliban, nor that he was a member of the Taliban.* . . . Is there anything in the Mobbs declaration that says Hamdi ever fired a weapon? . . . Without access to the screening criteria actually used by the government in its classification decision [declaring Hamdi an enemy combatant], this Court is unable to determine whether the government has paid adequate consideration to due process rights to which Hamdi is entitled." (Emphasis added.)

The Fourth Circuit Court of Appeals wholly ignored Judge Doumar's entirely legitimate constitutional scrutiny of the government's two pieces of paper purportedly proving the necessity of depriving this American citizen of his right to challenge the government's case against him. As Frank Dunham says of his client, "Nobody knows what his version of the facts might be."

Elisa Massimino, a director of the Lawyers Committee for Human Rights, makes this critical point in the January 9 *New York Times*: "[The Fourth Circuit] seems to be saying that it has no role whatsoever in overseeing the administration's conduct of the war on terrorism.

"That is particularly disturbing in the context of a potentially open-ended, as-yet-undeclared war, the beginning and end of which is left solely to the president's discretion."

In its report *A Year of Loss: Reexamining Civil Liberties Since September 11* (September 2002), the Lawyers Committee for Human Rights declared that in addition to many lives and our sense of invulnerability, "the United States has lost something essential and defining: some of the cherished principles on which the country is founded have been eroded or disregarded."

The Supreme Court is *our* court of last resort, as well as Hamdi's. While the Fourth Circuit did not say that what happened to Hamdi could be inflicted on an American citizen captured on American soil, constitutional law professor David Cole notes, "There would be some in the government who would claim that in this conflict the combat zone is the world."

On June 5, 2003, Attorney General John Ashcroft firmly told the House Judiciary Committee that the streets of America are "a war zone."

On July 9, the full Fourth Circuit Court of Appeals affirmed eight to four its earlier decision on Hamdi. Said dissenting judge Diana Gribbon Motz: "[The ruling] marks the first time in our history that a federal court has approved the elimination of protections afforded a citizen by the Constitution solely on the basis of the executive's designation of that citizen as an enemy combatant, without testing the accuracy of that designation." The Supreme Court will now decide.

CHAPTER TWELVE

Ashcroft's Detention Camps

Jonathan Turley is a professor of constitutional and public-interest law at George Washington University Law School in D.C. He is also a defense attorney in national security cases and other matters, writes for a number of publications, and is often on television. He and I occasionally exchange leads on civil liberties stories.

A Jonathan Turley column in the national edition of the August 14, 2002, *Los Angeles Times* ("Camps for Citizens: Ashcroft's Hellish Vision") begins: "Attorney General John Ashcroft's announced desire for camps for U.S. citizens he deems to be 'enemy combatants' has moved him from merely being a political embarrassment to being a constitutional menace." Actually, ever since General Ashcroft pushed the USA PATRIOT Act through an overwhelmingly supine Congress soon after September 11, he has subverted more elements of the Bill of Rights than any attorney general in American history.

It merits repeating that under the Justice Department's new definition of "enemy combatant"—which won the enthusiastic approval of the president and Defense Secretary Donald Rumsfeld—anyone defined as an "enemy combatant," very much including American citizens, can be held indefinitely by the government, without charges, a hearing, or a lawyer. In short, incommunicado. Among them: Yaser Hamdi and Jose Padilla.

As Harvard law professor Lawrence Tribe said on ABC's *Nightline* (August 12, 2002):

> It bothers me that the executive branch is taking the amazing position that just on the president's say-so, any American citizen can be picked up, not just in Afghanistan, but at O'Hare Airport or on the streets of any city in this country, and locked up without access to a lawyer or court just because the government says he's

connected somehow with the Taliban or Al-Qaeda. That's not the American way. It's not the constitutional way. . . . And no court can even figure out whether we've got the wrong guy.

Now more Americans are also going to be dispossessed of every fundamental legal right in our system of justice and put into camps. Jonathan Turley reports that Justice Department aides to General Ashcroft "have indicated that a 'high-level committee' will recommend which citizens are to be stripped of their constitutional rights and sent to Ashcroft's new camps."

It should be noted that Turley, who tries hard to respect due process, even in unpalatable situations, publicly defended Ashcroft during the latter's turbulent nomination battle, which is more than I did.

Again, in his *Los Angeles Times* column, Turley tries to be fair: "Of course Ashcroft is not considering camps on the order of the internment camps used to incarcerate Japanese American citizens in World War II. But he can be credited only with thinking smaller; *we have learned from painful experience that unchecked authority, once tasted, easily becomes insatiable.*" (Emphasis added.)

Turley has insisted that "the proposed camp plan should trigger immediate Congressional hearings and *reconsideration of Ashcroft's fitness for important office.* Whereas Al-Qaeda is a threat to the lives of our citizens, Ashcroft has become a clear and present threat to our liberties." (Emphasis added.) There has, as yet, been no Congressional call for such hearings.

On August 8, 2002, the *Wall Street Journal,* which much admires Ashcroft on its editorial pages, reported that "the Goose Creek, South Carolina, facility that houses [Jose] Padilla—mostly empty since it was designated in January to hold foreigners captured in the U.S. and facing military tribunals—now has a special wing that could be used to jail about twenty U.S. citizens if the government were to deem them enemy combatants, a senior administration official said." The Justice Department has told Turley that it has not denied this story. And space can be found in military installations for more "enemy combatants."

But once the camps are operating, can General Ashcroft be restrained from detaining—not in these special camps, but in regular lockups—any American investigated under suspicion of domestic terrorism under the new, elastic FBI guidelines for criminal investigations? From page 3 of these Ashcroft terrorism FBI guidelines, it's worth noting again that "The nature of the conduct engaged in by a [terrorist] enterprise will justify an inference that the standard [for opening a criminal justice investigation] is satisfied, *even if there are no known statements by participants that advocate or indicate planning for violence or other prohibited acts.*" (Emphasis added.) That conduct can be simply "intimidating" the government, according to the USA PATRIOT Act.

Returning to General Ashcroft's plans for American enemy combatants, an August 8, 2002, *New York Times* editorial—written before those plans were revealed—said: "The Bush administration seems to believe, on no good legal authority, that if it calls citizens combatants in the war on terrorism, it can imprison them indefinitely and deprive them of lawyers. This defiance of the courts repudiates two centuries of constitutional law and undermines the very freedoms that President Bush says he is defending in the struggle against terrorism."

Meanwhile, as the camps are being prepared, Terry McAuliffe and the pack of Democratic presidential aspirants were campaigning with hardly any reference to the constitutional crimes being committed by Bush and Ashcroft. As Supreme Court Justice Louis Brandeis prophesied: "The greatest menace to freedom is an inert people." And an inert Democratic leadership, let alone the Republican leadership.

CHAPTER THIRTEEN

The American Way of Torture

> American intelligence agents have been torturing terrorist sus-
> pects, or engaging in practices pretty close to torture. They have
> also been handing over suspects to countries, such as Egypt,
> whose intelligence agencies have a reputation for brutality.
>
> —*The Economist*, London, January 11, 2003

> The picture that emerges is of a brass-knuckled quest for infor-
> mation . . . in which the traditional lines between right and
> wrong, legal and inhumane, are evolving and blurred.
>
> —*Washington Post*, December 26, 2002

> U.S. officials who take part in torture, authorize it, or even close
> their eyes to it, can be prosecuted by courts anywhere in the
> world.
>
> —Kenneth Roth, Human Rights Watch

On December 26, 2002, Kenneth Roth, executive director of Human
Rights Watch, which reports on human rights abuses in some seventy
countries, wrote a letter to George W. Bush, with copies to Colin Pow-
ell, Donald Rumsfeld, and Condoleezza Rice:

> Human Rights Watch is deeply concerned by allegations
> of torture and other mistreatment of al Qaeda detainees
> described in the *Washington Post* ("U.S. Decries Abuse
> but Defends Interrogations") on December 26. The alle-
> gations, if true, would place the United States in violation
> of some of the most fundamental prohibitions of inter-
> national human rights law. . . . Torture is never permis-
> sible against anyone, whether in times of peace or war.

I have been collecting fragments of press reports of torture by

American intelligence agencies over the past year, but the *Washington Post* story was the first extensive, detailed account of what is going on at CIA facilities in the Bagram Air Base in Afghanistan. From the front page of the December 26, 2002, *Washington Post*, about the Bagram air base:

> Those who refuse to cooperate inside this secret CIA interrogation center are sometimes kept standing or kneeling for hours, in black hoods or spray-painted goggles, according to intelligence specialists familiar with CIA interrogation methods. At times, they are held in awkward, painful positions and deprived of sleep with a twenty-four-hour bombardment of lights—subject to what are known as "stress and duress" techniques.

These CIA facilities are closed to the press and other outsiders, including some other government agencies, the *Post* reports. Moreover, "According to Americans with direct knowledge and others who have witnessed the treatment, captives are often 'softened up' by MPs and U.S. Army Special Forces troops who beat them up and confine them in tiny rooms.

"The alleged terrorists are commonly blindfolded, and thrown into walls, bound in painful positions." Medication to alleviate pain is withheld. Or, as a source in the story notes "in a deadpan voice, 'pain control for wounded patients is a very subjective thing.'"

Says "an official who has supervised the capture and transfer of accused terrorists, 'If you don't violate someone's human rights some of the time, you probably aren't doing your job.'" Another official is quoted: "We don't kick the [expletive] out of them. We send them to other countries so *they* can kick the [expletive] out of them." The term for these transfers is "extraordinary renditions." There is, of course, no legal process; and among the foreign intelligence services who lend a brutal hand are those of Jordan, Egypt, and Morocco. At least once, torturers in Syria have been enlisted.

The *Washington Post* report by Dana Priest and Barton Gellman dutifully quotes National Security Council spokesman Sean

McCormack: "The United States is treating enemy combatants in U.S. government control, *wherever held*, humanely and in a manner consistent with the Third Geneva Convention of 1949." (Emphasis added.) Note the phrase "wherever held." Prisoners shipped to torturers in other countries remain under American control.

One official directly involved in these "renditions" to foreign torture chambers said in the *Washington Post*, "I do it . . . with my eyes open." According to the *Post*, another "Bush administration official said the CIA, in practice, is using a narrow definition of what counts as 'knowing' that a suspect has been tortured. 'If we're not there in the room, who is to say?' said one official conversant with recent reports of renditions."

The December 26 story was followed the next day by an editorial, "Torture Is Not an Option." It ended: "The critical first step for the administration is to clarify what tactics it is using and which are still off-limits. . . . The American people ought to know and ought to be able to respond through their representatives and through individual and organizational voices. It shouldn't be the administration's unilateral call." After all, "there are certain things democracies don't do, even under duress."

There has been only a scattered, brief follow-up in the press on this torture story, even though, as *The Economist* notes, "there seems little reason to doubt [its] veracity." Moreover, *The Economist*, which I read with care every week, adds (January 9, 2003): *"Although well documented, the account has produced official denials and only a desultory discussion among American commentators, who seem no keener to discuss the subject than the British and French were when the issue arose in Northern Ireland and Algiers."* (Emphasis added.)

There has been no quick, independent coverage, for example, in the *New York Times*, which reminds me of when the *Post*'s Bob Woodward and Carl Bernstein broke the Watergate story and the *Times* lagged far behind. The *Times* recovered then, but the recent "paper of record" is not consistently living up to its legendary past importance. It misses such stories as the *Post*'s on torture, and its editorials have become utterly predictable. The fault is not with the reporters. The decline began with the ascension of publisher Arthur

Sulzberger Jr. and it quickened under former executive editor Howell Raines. It's too bad the *New York Herald Tribune* isn't still around to challenge the *Times*.

But as for the American way of torture, Human Rights Watch is on the job, and Kenneth Roth will not let go. As Roth pertinently told the president: "The U.S. Department of State annual report on human-rights practices has frequently criticized torture in countries where detainees may have been sent. These include Uzbekistan, Pakistan, Egypt, Jordan, and Morocco. The United States thus could not plausibly claim that it was unaware of the problem of torture in these countries."

In June 2003, the president declared that, with regard to torture and any "cruel and unusual" abuses of "enemy combatants" and other prisoners, the United States pledges to adhere to international human rights law. Particular credit for this belated statement by the administration is due to the *Washington Post* and Human Rights Watch.

CHAPTER FOURTEEN

Our Designated Killers

The People are the only sure reliance for the preservation of our liberty.

—Thomas Jefferson

We have a choice. We can fight and win a just war against terrorism. . . . Or, we can win while running roughshod over the principles of fairness and due process that we claim to cherish, thus shaming ourselves in the eyes of the world and—eventually, when the smoke of fear and anger finally clears—in our own eyes as well.

—Bob Herbert, *New York Times*, December 3, 2001

The disciplined Bush administration strives continually to keep out of the news those of its security operations that are creating what the *Washington Post* accurately and ominously describes as an "alternative legal system," Or, as I call it, "a shadow Constitution."

Too often, the media are complicit in this secrecy because of their shallowness on constitutional issues, but sometimes they put sudden light on government orders and subsequent actions that were meant to remain deep in the shadows. This happened to the Rumsfeld-Poindexter Terrorism Information Awareness System that, because of press exposure, has now been blocked, for a time, in the Senate, by both Democratic and Republican legislators. They may have become aware that this all-seeing eye, out of 1984, could be looking into their own personal information.

But there has been little follow-up to this front-page story in the December 15, 2002, *New York Times*: "The Bush administration has prepared a list of terrorist leaders the Central Intelligence Agency [under George Tenet] is authorized to kill, if capture is impractical and civilian casualties can be minimized, senior military and intelligence officers said."

Acting on that presidential authorization, "a pilotless Predator aircraft operated [by the CIA] fired a Hellfire antitank missile" at a car in a remote region of Yemen, killing six, including an Al-Qaeda leader, Salim Sinan al-Harethi, and "one suspected Al-Qaeda operative with United States citizenship."

That dead American passenger was Kamal Derwish, who, according to the Bush administration, was the leader of an alleged cell of Al-Qaeda sleepers in Lackawanna, a Buffalo, New York, suburb. As syndicated columnist Charles Levendosky—a constant and accurate chronicler of the Bush shadow Constitution—wrote:

"[Derwish was labeled] an enemy combatant, but only after his death. . . . Derwish was never accused of any crime in a court of law. Essentially, he was killed because of the company he kept"—and it was too late for him to tell his side of the story. Further, as Seymour Hersh—who brought glaring sunlight to the My Lai massacre by American troops during the Vietnam War—reported in the December 23 and 30, 2002, *New Yorker*, "There is no indication that American or Yemeni officers knew in advance who was in the car with al-Harethi. . . .

"The Yemeni official told me that there was no thought of blocking the highway and attempting to capture al-Harethi and his passengers, because he had evaded earlier attempts. . . . The official said, 'From past experience, this was the most effective way.'"

Remote-controlled assassination sure does the job.

David Wise, a veteran expert on espionage and covert action, asked a question (*Time*, February 3, 2003) about the termination of Mr. Derwish that should have been on editorial pages around the nation: An American citizen not charged [with] or convicted of any crime was killed by a CIA Predator, targeted with the cooperation of the Pentagon (Donald Rumsfeld, CEO], and there was hardly a peep of protest in this country. Where is the outrage? . . . It seems unlikely that being zapped by the CIA is exactly the sort of due process that the Framers had in mind when they wrote the Constitution."

But aside from the *New York Times* story, which was not followed up in that paper, and the brief mentions by Levendosky, Hersh, and Wise, most Americans had almost no information about this sudden, summary execution of an American citizen and the others in the car. Nor have there been any wide-scale media investigations of the CIA's designated killers and how their hit lists are compiled. Also largely unreported is that it is not only the CIA that has official vigilantes.

In his *New Yorker* article "Manhunt: The Bush Administration's New Strategy in the War Against Terrorism" (December 23–30, 2002), Seymour Hersh reveals another lethal Bush administration directive that involves Donald Rumsfeld's Defense Department. How many of you have heard of a July 22 secret directive by the defense secretary, as Hersh notes, "ordering Air Force General Charles Holland, the four-star commander of Special Operations [Green Berets, Delta Force, the Navy Seals, the Seventy-fifth Ranger Regiment, et al.] to develop a plan ... to capture terrorists for interrogation, or if necessary, to kill them, not simply to arrest them in a law-enforcement exercise"?

Hersh quotes a Pentagon consultant: "We've created a culture in the Special Forces—twenty and twenty-one-year olds who need adult leadership. They're assuming [the military has] legal authority, and they'll do it—eagerly eliminate any target assigned to them. Eventually, the intelligence will be bad, and innocent people will be killed."

But since the Hersh article appeared, there's been little of depth in the media about these manhunters and there have been no full-scale investigations of the CIA's torturing of prisoners in secret interrogation centers on our military bases.

Dana Priest was one of the reporters who broke the torture story in the December 26 *Washington Post*. Recently, I asked her why there's been so little follow-up in the rest of the media. "It's hard," she said, "to keep a story going when there's no outrage, as in Congress"— where there have been no calls for hearings. Moreover, as Daniel Ellsberg told *Editor & Publisher* (January 27, 2003), "People in newspapers are reluctant to build on or give credit to someone else's scoop."

The ungenerous free press—handmaidens to the Bush administration's alternative legal system and shadow Constitution!

While I was chronicling the CIA's hit squads—and Donald Rumsfeld's plans for similar hunting expeditions for the Special Forces units under his jurisdiction—I came across a December 30 Associated Press report from Jerusalem that Israeli attorney general Elyakim

Rubinstein had instructed Prime Minister Ariel Sharon "to use the practice of killing suspected terror suspects [i.e., targeted assassinations] only as a last resort."

In the past, the Bush administration has criticized Sharon's having Palestinian terrorists targeted for summary execution—with occasional collateral deaths of innocent Palestinians caught in the line of fire.

But in this country, George W. Bush (as the December 15, 2002, *New York Times* reported) has authorized the CIA to kill terrorist leaders on an administration list—with, hopefully, minimum civilian casualties. Apparently, Sharon will no longer be admonished on this matter from Washington.

On the Shamash Web site (the Jewish Network) on December 20, there were excerpts from newspaper commentaries in twenty-five countries regarding, among other Bush directives, his "granting CIA authority to use lethal forces against suspected terrorists."

From the conservative Spanish publication *La Razón*, December 16: "It is alarming to see that the fear existing after 9/11, in the most powerful nation has blinded its leaders to such an extent that they would see as a good crime of the state, and to consider legal the execution, without previous trial, of people accused, by a discredited security service, of terrorism . . ."

In Pakistan, the center-right *Nation* editorialized on December 17 that the Bush administration's handing over "to the CIA a list of individuals, considered to be terrorists, with authorization to eliminate them physically . . . will relieve the CIA of the bother to seek approval to kill in each individual case. . . . Terrorism cannot be eliminated through terrorist methods."

The original *New York Times* report on the CIA's list of targets noted that "the presidential finding authorizing the president to kill terrorists was not limited to those on the list. The president has given broad authority to the CIA to kill or capture operatives of Al-Qaeda around the world, officials said." Quoted in the report was Harold Hongju Koh, a professor of international law at Yale and an official in the State Department during Bill Clinton's administration:

The inevitable complication of a politically declared but legally undeclared war [against terrorism] is the blurring of the distinction between enemy combatants and other nonstate actors. . . . The question is, what factual showing will demonstrate that they had warlike intentions against us, and who sees the evidence before any action is taken?

With rare journalistic enterprise, on January 11, 2003, Doyle McManus, Washington bureau chief of the *Los Angeles Times*, wrote a long analysis of this new expansion of the CIA's lethal authority ("A U.S. License to Kill"). He asked a crucial question: *"If the* CIA *kills more suspected terrorists in more countries, will it have the unintended effect of 'legitimizing' terror attacks against U.S. military officers in foreign countries or even at home?"* (Emphasis added.)

Furthermore, McManus continued, "where possible, the U.S. is seeking permission of local governments before carrying out targeted killings on foreign soil—although officials suggest that Bush is willing to waive that rule if necessary. Launching a targeted killing in another country without its assent is normally a violation of international law, legal scholars say.

"'There may be some cases where we can't make it conform to international law,' one official said [to McManus]. 'In that case, let's just make it conform to our law.'" Also quoted is Porter Goss (Republican, Florida), chairman of the House Intelligence Committee, who is concerned that the killing guidelines, the decision-making process, isn't yet clear enough. "That mechanism," he says, "still needs to be set up."

But the fundamental question, as McManus says, is whether Americans are ready "to accept targeted-killing missions . . . that kill clearly innocent civilians?"

I would add a further question: How will we know how many of these killing missions will take place, including how many of the dead are innocent civilians?

The congressional intelligence committees will presumably be informed of these missions, but in how much detail? And to what extent, if any, will American courts be involved in these targeted executions? As I pointed out at least one American citizen, in Yemen, has been terminated in one of these CIA missions. He was considered "an enemy combatant" but was never charged with any crime, nor was he brought into any court before his instant decease from a Hell-fire antitank missile fired from a pilotless Predator aircraft operated by the CIA.

Hardly reassuring is the news (*New York Times*, January 29, 2003) that the president is creating a Terrorist Threat Integration Center that will "merge units at the CIA, FBI, and other agencies into a single government unit intended to strengthen the collection and analysis of foreign and domestic terror threats." In charge of this spook fiefdom will be CIA Director George Tenet. For the first time, the CIA, which has often been its own private rogue government in the past, will have "full control over the collection and evaluation of all information relating to terrorist threats in the United States and overseas"—as well as control over responding to them.

Said an FBI official: "We just don't know what this [CIA hegemony] is going to mean." Neither do I. Who's going to tell the citizenry? Not Tenet or Bush.

And will Tenet be able to rein in Defense Secretary Donald Rumsfeld, who is planning to provide more funds, troops, and equipment to the Pentagon's shadowy Special Operations Forces, letting these commandos "run their own operations," including (as the January 6, 2003, *Washington Times* notes) the authority to "kill or capture terrorists around the world"?

Both the military and the CIA will greatly increase their already unprecedented powers in this borderless war, including at home. The Constitution calls for civilian control of the military, right?

CHAPTER FIFTEEN

Ashcroft's Master Plan to Spy on Us

Back home, one of the attorney general's most expansive—and alarming—plans to keep track of vast numbers of us Americans—was Operation TIPS—briefly noted in an earlier chapter.

The July 17, 2002, editorial in the *Boston Globe* was headlined "Ashcroft vs. Americans." It began: "Operation TIPS—the Terrorism Information and Prevention System—is a scheme that Joseph Stalin would have appreciated. Plans for its pilot phase, to start in August, would have Operation TIPS recruiting a million letter carriers, meter readers, cable technicians, and other workers with access to private homes as informants to report to the Justice Department any activities they think suspicious."

This newest John Ashcroft battle plan in the war on civil liberties would have us join the citizens of China, Cuba, Kazakhstan, and other countries where there is ubiquitous surveillance for signs of disloyalty to the state. Not only Joseph Stalin but also George Orwell would have understood what John Ashcroft had in mind. As the *Boston Globe* went on to say, "Ashcroft's informant corps is a vile idea not merely because it violates civil liberties . . . or because it will sabotage genuine efforts to prevent terrorism by overloading law enforcement officials with irrelevant reports about Americans who have nothing to do with terrorists. Operation TIPS should be stopped because it is utterly anti-American."

I was first alerted to Operation TIPS by Matt Olson in *Isthmus*, a lively alternative paper from Madison, Wisconsin. Then the May issue of *The Progressive*—a national monthly magazine also out of Madison—ran the full story by Bill Berkowitz, a regular contributor to www.workingforchange.com, Working Assets' site.

This time, John Ashcroft was so confident of public applause for his plan to smoke out the lurking terrorist "sleepers" among us that he didn't keep it secret. On May 29, 2002, on the government Web site www.citizencorps.gov/tips.html there it was! Meet Big Brother:

> A nationwide program giving millions of American truckers, letter carriers, train conductors, ship captains, utility employees, and others a formal way to report suspicious terrorist activity. Operation TIPS, a project of the U.S. Department of Justice, will begin as a pilot program in ten cities that will be selected.... Everywhere in America, a concerned worker can call a toll-free number and be connected directly to a hotline routing calls to the proper law enforcement agency or other responder organizations.

By July 16, that government Web site had removed the listing of specific kinds of worker-informants who would be watching us, but it noted that all the TIPsters had to do was "use their common sense and knowledge of their work environment to identify suspicious or unusual activity." There was no definition of "suspicious" or "unusual." The president endorsed Operation TIPS, as did Homeland Security's Tom Ridge and then Senate Republican Minority Leader Trent Lott. The ACLU, of course, opposed Operation TIPS.

As usual, there was no word of alarm from Tom Daschle or Dick Gephardt. But Democratic congressman Dennis Kucinich, ranking Democrat on the Government Oversight Committee's National Security Oversight Subcommittee, told Bill Berkowitz in *The Progressive*: "It appears we are being transformed from an information society to an informant society."

Where were Al Gore, John Edwards, John Kerry, Joe Lieberman, Charles Schumer, and Hillary Rodham Clinton?

Suddenly, however, Operation TIPS seemed to crash. On July 19, Ellen Sorokin reported in the *Washington Times* that a prominent conservative, "House Majority Leader Dick Armey, in his markup of legislation to create a Homeland Security Department ... scrapped a program that would use volunteers in domestic surveillance."

The Postal Service, in part because of the pressure from its unions, had already refused to permit its letter carriers to participate in Operation TIPS.

What follows is from Dick Armey's markup on the "Freedom and Security" section of the Homeland Security Bill. He wrote: "Because the [Homeland Security] Department has a singular mission of protecting the freedoms of Americans, specific legal protections will ensure that freedom is not undermined.... *Citizens Will Not Become Informants.* To ensure that no operation of the Department can be construed to promote citizens spying on one another, this draft will contain language to prohibit programs such as 'Operation TIPS.'"

Armey also canceled a cherished Bush-Ashcroft antiterrorism weapon, a national ID card. Wrote Armey: "The federal government will not have the authority to nationalize drivers' licenses and other ID cards. Authority to design and issue these cards shall remain with the states. The use of biometric identifiers and Social Security numbers with these cards is not consistent with a free society."

Also, Armey—described in *The Almanac of American Politics 2002* as often driving a pickup truck, wearing cowboy boots, and quoting country music lyrics—established, in his markup of the Homeland Security Bill, "A Privacy Officer. Working as a close adviser to the Secretary, this officer will ensure technology research and new regulations from the Department respect the civil liberties our citizens enjoy. *This is the first-ever such officer established by law in a cabinet department.*" (Emphasis added).

Despite Dick Armey's rejection of the Bush-Ashcroft plan for what conservative Republican Bob Barr calls an official "snitch system," the Department of Justice declared that Operation TIPS would continue. I called Ashcroft's spokeswoman, Barbara Comstock, and she explained that since the Senate was still debating its version of the Homeland Security Bill, Armey's revisions had not become law; and until—if and when—they are enacted, Operation TIPS would go forward. But it was eventually stopped—for the time being.

CHAPTER SIXTEEN

The Apparent Death
of Operation TIPS

When the Homeland Security Act was finally signed by the president in November 2002, after many weeks of extensive media coverage of the congressional warfare over the bill, I saw nothing of the most significant result of it all—the decision to ban what had been a key provision.

> Section 880. Prohibition of the Terrorism Information and Prevention System—Any and all activities of the Federal Government to implement the proposed component program of the Citizen Corps known as Operation TIPS (Terrorism Information and Prevention System) *are hereby prohibited.* (Emphasis added.)

Democratic Senator Patrick Leahy of Vermont had tried months before to get Operation TIPS out of the Senate version of the bill, but Joe Lieberman, chair of the Governmental Affairs Committee, ignored his letter asking for the killing of the nationwide governmental surveillance program.

Dick Armey, who had previously killed Operation TIPS in the House, eventually prevailed because the Senate did essentially pass the House version of the bill, including Armey's elimination of Operation TIPS. When the congressional battlefield was cleared, Pat Leahy released a statement on November 19, which—so far as I have seen— has been ignored by the media: "I am pleased the bill, in section 880, forbids the creation of Operation TIPS." Leahy noted that originally, the Justice Department had described the operation as "giving millions of American truckers, letter carriers, train conductors, ship captains, utility employees, and others a formal way to report suspicious

... activity." Or, as the department's Web site put it, "potentially terrorist-related activity."

After strong protests around the country, TIPS was reportedly scaled back somewhat; but, as Leahy said, before the plan failed to pass Congress, "it was unclear whether these changes reflected actual changes in the Justice Department's plans, or whether they were simply cosmetic differences designed to blunt opposition to the program."

At no time did the Justice Department indicate how it planned to train this horde of amateur spies. Accordingly, as Leahy emphasized, "such a setup could have allowed unscrupulous participants to abuse their new status to place innocent neighbors under undue scrutiny." Much worse yet, the names of these innocent suspects would be transferred by the Justice Department to FBI, CIA, and other government databases that are now permitted to exchange "intelligence" information under the Homeland Security Act.

At one point, a source inside the Justice Department told me that not only was Operation TIPS not Ashcroft's idea, but Ashcroft was uncomfortable with the project. Being a team player, he never criticized this national-spying corps plan publicly, so the source said.

Interestingly, there was a time when Ashcroft appeared to be somewhat of a libertarian on privacy rights. Thanks to Matt Drudge's Web site (www.drudgereport.com), I have a copy of a 1997 statement by then Senator John Ashcroft, chairman of the Senate Commerce Subcommittee on Consumer Affairs, Foreign Commerce, and Tourism. Titled "Keep Big Brother's Hands Off the Internet," the release by Ashcroft sounds like it was written by the ACLU:

> The protections of the Fourth Amendment are clear. The right to protection from unlawful searches is an *indivisible American value*. Two hundred years of court decisions have stood in defense of this fundamental right. *The state's interest in crime-fighting should never vitiate the citizens' Bill of Rights.* (Emphasis added.)

Yet, as attorney general of the United States, however, Ashcroft has rewritten much of the Bill of Rights in the USA PATRIOT Act, and has unilaterally eviscerated the First, Fifth, and Sixth Amendments and Fourth Amendment privacy rights, in other actions.

Moreover, in Ashcroft's proposed sequel to the USA PATRIOT Act, as will be shown in a later chapter, Operation TIPS has been partially resurrected.

CHAPTER SEVENTEEN

Ashcroft Out of Control

Many of the new security measures proposed by our government in the name of fighting the "war on terror" are not temporary. They are permanent changes to our laws. Even the measures that, on the surface, appear to have been adopted only as long as the war on terror lasts, could be with us indefinitely. Because, as Homeland Security director Tom Ridge himself has warned, terrorism is a "permanent condition to which America must . . . adjust."

—American Civil Liberties Union, January 29, 2003

The battle to protect the Constitution keeps adding new and more dangerous dimensions. On February 7, 2003, Charles Lewis, head of the Washington-based Center for Public Integrity, received a secret, but not classified, Justice Department draft of a bill that would expand the already unprecedented government powers to restrict civil liberties authorized by the USA PATRIOT Act. This new bill is called the Domestic Security Enhancement Act of 2003. Lewis, in an act of patriotism—since this still is a constitutional democracy—put the eighty-six page draft on the center's Web site (www.publicintegrity.org).

On the evening of February 7, Charles Lewis discussed this new assault on our fundamental liberties on Bill Moyers's PBS program, *Now*. Three days later, on the editorial page of the daily *New York Sun*, primarily a conservative newspaper, Errol Louis wrote: "[The] document is a catalog of authoritarianism that runs counter to the basic tenets of modern democracy."

I have the entire draft of the bill. Section 201 would overturn a federal court decision that ordered the Bush administration to reveal the identities of those it has detained (imprisoned) since 9/11. This sequel to the USA PATRIOT Act states that "the government need *not* disclose information about individuals detained in investigations of terrorism until . . . the initiation of criminal charges."

Many of the prisoners caught in the Justice Department's initial dragnet were held for months without charges or contact with their families, who didn't know where they were. And these prisoners were often abused by the guards and out of reach of their lawyers—if they'd been able to find a lawyer before being shifted among various prisons. When, after much pressure, the Justice Department released the numbers of the imprisoned, there were no names attached until a lower court decided otherwise.

Under the proposed Ashcroft bill, for the first time in U.S. history, secret arrests will be specifically permitted. That section of bill is flatly titled "Prohibition of Disclosure of Terrorism Investigation Detainee Information." In Argentina, those secretly taken away were known as "the disappeared." On June 17, 2003, the District of Columbia Court of Appeals agreed with what Ashcroft advocates, but the Supreme Court has yet to rule on the constitutionality of secret arrests.

Moving on, under Section 501 of the blandly titled Domestic Security Enhancement Act of 2003, an American *citizen* can be stripped of citizenship if he or she "becomes a member of, or provides material support to, a group that the United States has designated as a 'terrorist organization,' if that group is engaged in hostilities against the United States."

Until now, in our law, an American could only lose his or her citizenship by declaring a clear intent to abandon it. But—and read this carefully from the new bill—"the intent to relinquish nationality need not be manifested in words, but can be *inferred* from conduct." (Emphasis added).

Who will do the "inferring"? A member of the Justice Department. Not to worry. As John Ashcroft's spokeswoman, Barbara Comstock, says of objections to this draft "Son of Patriot" bill, "The [Justice] department's deliberations are always undertaken with the strongest commitment to our Constitution and civil liberties." (This is a faith-based administration.)

What this section of the bill actually means is that if you provide "material support" to an organization by sending a check for its *legal* activities—not knowing that it has been designated a "terrorist" group for other things it does—you can be stripped of your citizenship and be detained indefinitely as an alien. While South Africa was ruled by an apartheid government, certain activities of the African National Congress were categorized as "terrorist," but many Americans provided support to the legal antiapartheid work of that organization.

Under Section 302 of John Ashcroft's design for our future during the indefinite war on terrorism, there is another change in our legal system. Under current law, the FBI can collect DNA identification records of persons convicted of various crimes. But under the new bill, the "attorney general or secretary of defense" will be able to "collect, analyze, and maintain DNA samples" of "suspected terrorists." And as Georgetown law professor David Cole notes, "mere association" will be enough to involve you with suspected terrorist groups. What does "association" mean? For one thing, "material support," under which you could lose your citizenship.

In reaction to the stealth with which the Justice Department has been crafting this invasion of the Bill of Rights, Democratic Senator Patrick Leahy of Vermont, ranking minority member of the Senate Judiciary Committee, said on February 10: "The early signals from the administration about its intentions for this bill are ominous. . . . For months, and as recently as just last week, Justice Department officials have denied to members of the Judiciary Committee that they were drafting another antiterrorism package. There still has not been any hint from them about their draft bill."

Leahy continued: "The contents of this proposal should be carefully reviewed, and the public must be allowed to freely engage in any debate about the merits of any new government powers the administration may seek." But there was little follow-up in the media on the radical revisions of our liberties in "Patriot Act II."

CHAPTER EIGHTEEN

Red Alert for the Bill of Rights

The Justice Department . . . seems to be running amok. . . . This agency right now is the biggest threat to personal liberty in the country.

—Republican conservative Dick Armey, former House majority leader, *New Republic*, October 21, 2002

This nation . . . has no right to expect that it always will have wise and humane rulers, sincerely attached to the principles of the Constitution . . . [If] the calamities of war again befall us, the dangers to human liberty are frightful to contemplate.

—United States Supreme Court, *Ex Parte Milligan*, 1866, declaring Abraham Lincoln's suspension of *habeas corpus* and other abuses of the Bill of Rights unconstitutional

We may never know the name of the patriot who leaked John Ashcroft's draft of the Domestic Security Enhancement Act, a sequel to the USA PATRIOT Act, to Charles Lewis, head of the Center for Public Integrity. This broke the story of the most radical government plan in our history to remove from Americans their liberties under the Bill of Rights.

As the *Washington Post* warned in a February 12, 2003, editorial, this proposed law—prepared in secret for months while the Justice Department told Congress it had no such legislation in mind—gives the Bush administration "more power unilaterally to exempt people from the protections of the justice system and place them in a kind of alternative legal world."

On Bill Moyers's program, Charles Lewis said it took "the most incredible kind of courage" for a member of the Justice Department to have leaked this draft. "There's gonna be a witch-hunt," Lewis predicted. "[If found, the leaker] could very likely not only lose their job, but . . . be ruined professionally. [And I] have an incredible respect for anyone who does that."

Called the Domestic Security Enhancement Act (DSEA) of 2003, the legislation, as I noted, was most likely intended to be sprung on Congress and the rest of us once the war on Iraq began. As Charles Levendosky, editorial page editor of the Casper, Wyoming, *Star-Tribune*, said in his syndicated column (February 24, 2003) :

> The DSEA isn't a working paper. It's a complete proposal for legislation. One cannot escape the ramifications. The thoroughness of DSEA is meant to discourage congressional changes, deletions, or amendments. . . . It attacks the fundamental framework of our democracy by removing the checks and balances that hold it together and make it work.

In addition to the judiciary and Congress, the other check the Framers relied on to stop uncontrolled government power was what used to be called the Fourth Estate. That's why the First Amendment guarantees "Congress shall make no law . . . abridging the . . . freedom . . . of the press." But most of the media treated this unprecedented revision of the Constitution as a one- or two-day story, and there was scant mention of it on television. Interestingly, the largest response soon after Bill Moyers's February 7 interview with Charles Lewis was from 3,581 radio stations informing their listeners. And Moyers's Web site got more than two hundred thousands citizen hits after the interview.

But as happened with the *Washington Post*'s front-page story on the torture of prisoners in CIA interrogation at our military bases overseas—and the *Los Angeles Times*' detailed report on the CIA's targeted killings—there has been little follow-up in newspapers or on broadcast and cable television.

Aldous Huxley once wrote of our "almost infinite appetite for distraction," and that attention deficit has increasingly characterized the effect on the press of the twenty-four-hour news-cycle race. I wonder what the job qualifications are these days for assignment editors.

But for the media, and anyone else, the American Civil Liberties Union prepared a nineteen-page, single-spaced, section-by-section analysis of the myriad constitutional violations in the DSEA. The ACLU released a similar, invaluable dissection of the first USA PATRIOT Act, but very little of that appeared in the media. And to this day, not many Americans know what's in that omnivorous law—let alone how it's being implemented.

The ACLU analysis of DSEA was written by legislative counsel Timothy Edgar. In his initial summary, Edgar notes that this bill, if signed into law by the eager president, would, among other consequences, "threaten public health by severely restricting access to crucial information about environmental health risks posed by facilities that use dangerous chemicals."

Also, the law would "allow for the sampling and cataloguing of innocent Americans' genetic information *without court order and without consent*" and "permit, without any connection to antiterrorism efforts, sensitive personal information about U.S. citizens to be shared with local and state law enforcement." (Emphasis added.)

And, although Operation TIPS has been canceled—thanks to Dick Armey when he was majority leader of the House—the Justice Department doesn't give up easily. This new bill, the ACLU points out, would provide "an incentive for neighbor to spy on neighbor, and pose problems similar to those inherent in Attorney General Ashcroft's 'Operation TIPS,' by granting blanket immunity to businesses that phone in false terrorism TIPS, even if their actions are taken with reckless disregard for the truth."

And, for those who remember the stunningly illegal orders given to government officials by Richard Nixon, the proposed bill will "shelter federal agents engaged in illegal surveillance—without a court order—from criminal prosecution if they are following orders of High Executive Branch officials." Trust the White House!

In 1771, Sam Adams wrote in the *Boston Gazette:* "Power . . . intoxicates the mind; and unless those with whom it is entrusted are carefully watched," such men will not govern the people "according to the known laws of the state." How intently will Congress be watching "Patriot Act II" or "Patriot Act III"?

CHAPTER NINETEEN

The Sons and Daughters of Liberty and Their Opponents

In 1756, in Boston and other cities and towns, the coming of the American Revolution was speeded by mechanics, merchants, and artisans who organized against British tyranny. Calling themselves the Sons of Liberty, they later set up Committees of Correspondence in the colonies to spread detailed news about British attacks on their liberties. They focused on the general search warrant, which allowed customs officers to invade and ransack their homes and offices at will.

In the spirit of the Sons of Liberty, on February 4, 2002, some four hundred citizens of Northampton, Massachusetts, held a town meeting to organize ways to—as they put it—protect the residents of the town from the Bush-Ashcroft USA PATRIOT Act. On that night, the Northampton Bill of Rights Defense Committee began a new American Revolution. Similar committees have since been organizing around the country.

Speakers at that first town meeting were defying John Ashcroft, who threatened dissenters in his testimony before the Senate Judiciary Committee last year. He denounced those "who scare peace-loving people with phantoms of lost liberty.... Your tactics only aid terrorists, for they erode our national unity and diminish our resolve. They give ammunition to America's enemies."

But speakers at the meeting emphasized that the USA PATRIOT Act and the succession of unilateral Ashcroft-Bush orders that followed apply not only to noncitizens but also to Americans in that very hall. William Newman, director of the ACLU of Western Massachusetts, pointed out that law enforcement agencies are now permitted "the same access to your Internet use and to your e-mail use that they had to your telephone records"—and may overstep their authority. "The history of the FBI," Newman warned, "is that they will do exactly that."

Also speaking was University of Massachusetts professor Bill Strickland, whom I first met when he directed the Northern Student Movement during the civil rights campaigns of the 1950s and 1960s. Said Strickland, "The elements of the PATRIOT Act place all of us in danger."

One result of that meeting was a petition, signed by more than one thousand Northamptonites, urging the city government to approve a "resolution to defend the Bill of Rights." Thanks to a persistent organizing drive, that resolution passed the Northampton City Council by a unanimous vote on May 2, 2002. It targets not only the USA PATRIOT Act but also all subsequent actions by Ashcroft and others that "threaten key rights guaranteed to U.S. citizens and noncitizens by the Bill of Rights and the Massachusetts Constitution."

Among those key rights are "freedom of speech, assembly, and privacy; the right to counsel and due process in judicial proceedings; and protection from unreasonable searches and seizures."

The city of Northampton officially asks, from now on, that "federal and state law enforcement report to the local Human Rights Commission all local investigations undertaken under aegis of the [USA PATRIOT] Act and Orders; and that the community's congressional representatives actively monitor the implementation of the Act and Orders, and work to repeal those sections found unconstitutional."

This is a signal to the mostly passive members of Congress that actual voters are watching them.

In April 2002, similar resolutions to defend the Bill of Rights from the Bush administration and from complicit members of Congress afraid to challenge Ashcroft were passed in the nearby towns of Amherst and Leverett. The city councils of Ann Arbor, Michigan, and Berkeley, California, passed civil liberties resolutions in January, as did the Denver, Colorado, city council in March and the city council in Cambridge, Massachusetts, on June 17. Other cities have kept coming aboard.

You would think this grassroots movement to secure our liberties would be of interest to the national media, but I have seen little of it on television or in the print press.

At the town meeting in Leverett, Massachusetts, Don Ogden, who initiated the resolution, noted—and I hope the FBI transmits this to John Ashcroft—that "it is truly Orwellian doublespeak to call such unpatriotic efforts a 'patriot act.'"

In Amherst, Massachusetts, as the town council passed a similar resolution, Select Board Person Ann Awad did not at all see John Ashcroft's "phantoms of lost liberty." They are real to her. "As members of the Select Boards" she said, "we want to know that all residents and visitors to our town feel safe. We do not want to support profiling of particular types of people. If one group is viewed suspiciously today another group will be added to the list tomorrow."

Meanwhile, the citizens of Northampton are well aware of what constitutional lawyer David Cole wrote in the valuable "Striking Back" issue of *The Nation* (June 3, 2002):

> National-security types often assure us that wartime diminutions of civil liberties are only temporary. But this is likely to be a permanent war. Defense Secretary Donald Rumsfeld has said that the war will not be over— and the prisoners on Guantánamo will not be released— until there are no terrorists organizations of potentially global reach left in the world.
>
> Given that modern technology gives practically everyone 'global reach,' that day will never come.... The only certainty is that we will see further erosions of our privacy, our freedoms, and our principles.

Also in that issue of *The Nation* is an ominous and revealing article by Robert Dreyfuss ("The Cops Are Watching You"), which details the increasing interconnections among the FBI, state and local intelligence units, and antiterrorism squads. For one example, there is veteran FBI agent Mike Clemens, now stationed in Baltimore, who assembles and directs Maryland's FBI Joint Terrorism Task Force (JTTF). To determine which groups under surveillance might be involved in violent activity, Clemens told Dreyfuss, a wide spectrum of organizations has to be monitored.

Therefore, writes Dreyfuss, "the FBI—working in conjunction with state and local police—often gathers a significant amount of information on groups that end up having no proclivity towards violence, Clemens says. . . . 'We identify a group, develop sources inside it. Maybe we make fifteen contacts or more over a period of six months, and if they are all negative, we just leave them alone.'" This infiltration by multiple government forces is going on nationally.

And are the names of covertly surveilled group members, along with their other affiliations, eventually expunged from FBI files? That's as likely as George W. Bush doing penance for executing all those people while he was governor of Texas.

Keep in mind that this invasive FBI monitoring of entirely lawful groups was going on—under the direction of John Ashcroft—for months before he disclosed in May 2002 that, under the "new" guidelines, he was bringing back COINTELPRO (though he never used that disgraced name).

In his *Nation* article, Robert Dreyfuss also reports that in March 2002, the ACLU in Denver found out that *since* 1999, the police there "have maintained intelligence dossiers on 3,200 people in 208 organizations, from globalization protesters to the [Quaker] American Friends Service Committee, and from Amnesty International to the Chiapas Coalition and the American Indian Movement. 'Individuals who are not even suspected of a crime and organizations that don't have a criminal history are labeled criminal extremists,' says Mark Silverstein, legal director of the ACLU of Colorado." Under pressure from the ACLU of Colorado and the media, the police have ceased such surveillance.

That kind of government surveillance—greatly intensified after 9/11—is one of the reasons the Bill of Rights Defense Committees are increasing.

In *From Resistance to Revolution: Colonial Radicals and the Development of American Opposition to Britain, 1765-1776*, first published in 1974, historian Pauline Maier quotes a letter from Sam Adams emphasizing that "the colonists must henceforth depend primarily upon themselves for the defense of their liberties."

In another passage, published in the January 21, 1771, *Boston*

Gazette, and just as crucial and pertinent under Bush and Ashcroft as it was under King George III, Sam Adams wrote, "Our ship is in the hands of pilots who . . . are steering directly under full sail to a rock. The whole crew may see [this course to violate our liberties] in full view if they *look the right way*."

There is much more of value to our present condition in Pauline Maier's *From Resistance to Revolution*. Fortunately, this account of how American liberties were won has been put back in print by W. W. Norton & Co. I recommend the book highly to the Bill of Rights Defense Committees rising around the country, to ACLU affiliates, and to the growing number of increasingly concerned citizens—from right to left and in the middle.

The book's epigraph is from Alexis de Tocqueville's *Democracy in America* (1835): "The Revolution of the United States was the result of a mature and reflecting preference for freedom. . . . It contracted no alliance with the turbulent passions of anarchy, but its course was marked, on the contrary, by a love of order and law."

The Bush administration and the Democratic and Republican leaders of Congress keep intoning the mantra "the rule of law," while the FBI and CIA are amassing more information on more of us—traducing the law and using more invasive technology than ever before.

As Georgetown University law professor David Cole says, "Popular resistance is critical."

CHAPTER TWENTY

Grass Roots of the Constitution

The growing number of critics—from liberals to conservatives—of what they call John Ashcroft's war on the Bill of Rights—now includes former Manhattan United States Attorney Mary Jo White. This tough prosecutor, during her term, indicted Osama bin Laden for the U.S. embassy bombings in Africa and convicted more than thirty terrorists. Speaking before the New York City Bar Association, she questioned—as reported in the *New York Daily News*—Ashcroft's policies such as detaining immigrants in secret proceedings. "Secrecy," she said, "is the enemy of democracy."

But most remarkable in the rising resistance around the nation to Ashcroft's far-reaching expansion of electronic surveillance—and lowering of judicial supervision in some of his edicts—is the ferment at the grassroots.

Characteristic of most of these official disagreements with the attorney general is the Madison, Wisconsin, City Council instruction that local police and prosecutors not be drawn into activities that threaten the constitutional rights of area residents—such as random surveillance based on country of origin and fishing through library records to see what books people under vague suspicion of terrorist links are borrowing.

Simultaneously, the American Civil Liberties Union declares that, as part of this campaign, it will "work with dozens of communities around the country to go on the record against repressive legislation."

Laura Murphy, director of the ACLU's Washington Legislative Office, points out, "Local governments have the power to tell their law enforcement officers not to spy without evidence of crime. With the help of ACLU members and activists around the country, we will encourage them to say 'no' as strongly as possible to other violations of the Bill of Rights."

The legacy of all these committees that defend the Bill of Rights stems back, as I've detailed, to the pre–American Revolutionary Committees of Correspondence, which as Mercy Otis Warren writes in 1805 "supported a chain of communication from New Hampshire to Georgia that produced unanimity and energy throughout the continent."

Now, largely through the Internet, contemporary Committees of Correspondence—though not achieving "unanimity" among Americans—are encouraging more citizens to question whether the Bush administration is indeed securing the liberties we are fighting to protect from the terrorists. As a high school student told the Madison, Wisconsin, City Council: "We need to be more than passive observers of history, because the decisions made right now are our future."

A continuing recruiting source for committees across the country is the original Bill of Rights Defense Committee in Florence, Massachusetts (www.bordc.org). It provides a running score of registers and "tools" for further organizing anywhere.

With more than 130 towns, cities, or county councils—as well as three states—passing resolutions in defiance of Bush and Ashcroft, I've been asked whether these acts aren't really only symbolic. What can town and city councils across the country actually do to rein in the FBI, the CIA, and all the other intelligence agencies now interconnected through the Homeland Security Act of 2002?

A useful way to answer this pivotal question was reported on November 26, 2002, in the Eugene, Oregon, *Register-Guard*: "Eugene city councilors gave in to a stampede of constituents Monday night, surprising even themselves by voting unanimously at an impassioned meeting to make Eugene the next city in the United States and the fifteenth in Oregon to formally seek reform or repeal of the USA PATRIOT Act."

Said City Councilor Bonny Bettman: "We shouldn't stand by silently as those rights and freedoms are eroded. Our rights and freedoms really help distinguish us from our enemies."

This is Section 1 of *A Resolution of the City of Eugene Defending the Bill of Rights and Civil Liberties*:

> We ask that the U.S. Attorney's Office, the Office of the
> Federal Bureau of Investigation, the Oregon State Police,

and any other federal [and] state law enforcement officials and local law enforcement . . . report to the Eugene City Council and Human Rights Commission monthly and publicly the extent and manner in which they have acted under the USA PATRIOT Act and new executive orders, including but not limited to disclosing:

The names of any detainees held in the area or any Eugene residents detained here or elsewhere, the circumstances that led to the detention. The charges, if any, lodged against any detainees. The name of counsel, if any, representing each detainee.

The number of search warrants that have been executed in the City of Eugene—without notice to the subject of the warrant—pursuant to Section 213 of the USA PATRIOT Act. The extent of electronic surveillance carried out in the City of Eugene under powers granted in the USA PATRIOT Act.

The extent to which federal authorities are monitoring political meetings, religious gatherings, or other such activities within the City of Eugene. The number of times education records have been obtained from public schools and institutions of higher learning in the City of Eugene under Section 507 of the USA PATRIOT Act.

The number of times library records have been obtained from libraries under Section 215 of the USA PATRIOT Act. The number of times that records of the books purchased by store patrons from bookstores have been obtained in the City of Eugene under Section 215 of the USA PATRIOT Act; and subpoenas issued to Eugene citizens . . . without a court's approval or knowledge.

We resolve that, to the greatest extent legally possible, no city resources, particularly administrative or law enforcement funds, will be used for unconstitutional activities conducted under the USA PATRIOT Act or recent executive orders which permit activities listed above.

As Thomas Jefferson said in a December 26, 1820, letter to the Marquis de Lafayette: "The disease of liberty is catching." He also said, in a letter to Abigail Adams: "The spirit of resistance is so valuable on certain occasions, that I wish it to be always kept alive."

As Joe Mosely reported in the Eugene, Oregon, *Register Guard* on November 26, 2002, "more than two hundred people packed the council chamber and dozens more spilled out of its doorways as opponents to the sweeping antiterrorism act dominated an extended public comment session with testimony of lost liberties, ideals in peril, and a heartfelt fear of unchecked government." The disease of liberty was certainly catching.

> "My community was silenced; our voice is silent," said twenty-year-old Alexander Gonzales, a Hispanic student at the University of Oregon and lifelong Eugene resident. "We're afraid. I really can't express through words the fear that goes on."
>
> Others also told of feeling targeted by the PATRIOT Act—not because of their politics but due to national heritage, religious beliefs, or skin color. "I have not done anything; I am not a terrorist," said Nadia Sindi, a Muslim woman well-known in city and county circles as a land use activist. "I urge you to pass this resolution, for all of us."
>
> And Muhammed Kahn, a doctor who is new to Eugene, said he not only loves his new city but embraces the U.S. Constitution—whose ideals he described as close to those espoused by the Quran, Islam's holy book. "I just want to quote Benjamin Franklin, who said those who give up liberty for security deserve neither," Kahn said.
>
> Going into the meeting, at least half of the eight councilors were on record opposing a resolution—favoring instead a less formal letter that could be signed by individual councilors, stating their personal views rather than an official city position. But citizens on Monday

told the Council that's not enough. "Writing a simple letter would be crawling, rather than standing," Dawn Balzano Peebles said. "I've heard the fear in people's voices. I've heard the shaking in their spirits. Ordinary citizens are now fearful of their own government." One by one, those councilors opposed to a resolution joined the fold.

CHAPTER TWENTY-ONE

The Unilateral President

From September 11, 2001, on, the Bush administration has increasingly bypassed, sometimes secretly, the separation of powers that is at the core of our constitutional system of government. Attorney General John Ashcroft has been reluctant to answer Congressional questions on the implementation of the USA PATRIOT Act, and the administration's unilateral executive orders. And at times, he and other administration officials have not consulted Congress at all—until press accounts forced them to acknowledge at least to some extent, the role of Congress.

In the courts, the administration has maintained that in certain national security cases—particularly of "enemy combatants" who are also United States citizens—the courts must defer to the president's powers to protect the nation during the war on terrorism. At one point, Assistant Attorney General Michael Chertoff, head of the Justice Department's criminal division, said: "When we are talking about preventing acts of war against us, the judicial model does not work."

The Bush team, however, has yet to match Abraham Lincoln's expansion of the authority of the president to limit constitutional rights in time of war. It's useful, however, to consider the Lincoln presidency in this regard, because Bush's administration is assuming much of Lincoln's attitude, and arguments.

Lincoln suspended *habeas corpus* (anyone imprisoned must have the right to have a court determine whether that imprisonment is legally justified).

When James Madison was drafting sections of the Constitution, Thomas Jefferson strongly urged him to ensure that the writ of *habeas corpus* be in the main body of the Constitution, where indeed it is.

But, as Samuel Eliot Morison and Henry Steele Commager wrote in *The Growth of the American Republic* (Oxford University Press, 1942), during the Civil War, *military officers* "began to arrest persons suspected of disloyalty or espionage, and to confine them without trial in military prisons, for indefinite terms . . .

> A Maryland judge who had charged a grand jury to inquire into illegal acts of government officials was set upon by soldiers when his court was in session, beaten and dragged bleeding from his bench, and *imprisoned for six months* . . .
>
> Simultaneously with the Emancipation Proclamation, the President issued an order that seemed to deny white citizens the liberty he proposed to accord to Negro slaves. He proclaimed that all persons resisting the draft, discouraging enlistment, or "guilty of any disloyal practice affording aid and comfort to rebels" would be subject to martial law, tried by court martial [in military tribunals] and denied the writ of *habeas corpus*. (Emphasis added.)

Eric Foner, in *The Story of American Freedom* (W. W. Norton, 1998), added that during Lincoln's presidency, "arbitrary arrests by military authorities in the North . . . numbered in the thousands, ranging from opposition newspaper editors and Democratic politicians to ordinary civilians like the Chicago man briefly imprisoned for calling the president a 'damned fool.'"

Moreover, as to doing away with the writ of *habeas corpus* and holding prisoners without charges, "Lincoln claimed that right under the presidential war powers, and twice suspended the writ throughout the entire Union for those accused of 'disloyal activities.'"

When Lincoln's right to abolish the rights of dissenting American citizens was argued before the Supreme Court—after the Civil War was over, and Lincoln had been assassinated—the lawyer for the government told the Court that during wartime, presidential powers "must be without limit."

As for those parts of the Bill of Rights that had also been suspended—the First, Fourth, Fifth, and Sixth Amendments to the Constitution—Lincoln's lawyer argued that they were "peace provisions," which had to be put aside when, in wartime, "*salus populi suprema est lex*" (the people's welfare is the supreme law).

Writing for the majority of the Supreme Court, Justice David Davis scorned the government's argument that martial law and military tribunals were thoroughly justified to keep the nation safe. Said Justice Davis, according to that point of view, "It could well be said that a country, preserved at the sacrifice of all the cardinal principles of liberty, is not worth the cost of preservation."

The case, *Ex parte Milligan* (1866), resulted in a landmark decision that goes to the very essence of American constitutional democracy. It should be read while keeping in mind how John Ashcroft and other members of the Bush administration deal with the Bill of Rights and other parts of the Constitution.

Said the Supreme Court: "No graver question was ever considered in this court, nor one which more nearly concerns the rights of the whole people; for it is the birthright of every American citizen when charged with crime, to be tried and punished according to law ... *The Constitution of the United States is a law for rulers and people, equally in war and in peace, and covers with the shield of its protection all classes of men, at all times, and under all circumstances.* (Emphasis added.)

"No doctrine, involving more pernicious consequences, was ever invented by the wit of man than that any of [the Constitution's] provisions can be suspended during any of the great exigencies of government." Such a doctrine, said the Court, "leads directly to anarchy or despotism, but the theory of necessity on which it is based is false; for the Government, *within the Constitution,* has all the powers granted to it, which are necessary to preserve its existence ... (Emphasis added.)

"This nation, as experience has proved, cannot always remain at peace, and has no right to expect that it will always have wise and humane rulers, sincerely attached to the principles of the Constitution." If, the Court continued, "the calamities of war again befall us," and the Constitution is again bypassed, "the dangers to human liberty are frightful to contemplate.

"The Framers of the Constitution knew—the history of the world told them—the nation they were founding, be its existence short or long, would be involved in war; how often or how long continued, human foresight could not tell; and that unlimited power, wherever lodged at such a time, was especially hazardous to freemen.

"For this, and other equally weighty reasons, they secured the inheritance they had fought to maintain, by incorporating in a written constitution the safeguards which time had proved were essential to its preservation. *Not one of these safeguards can the President, or Congress, or the Judiciary disturb . . .*" (Emphasis added.)

But *habeas corpus* could be disturbed, the Court went on—*only* if the civilian courts were not open, and they were open during the Civil War. They are still open now, but the Bush administration is denying American citizens, designated "enemy combatants" solely by the president, the essentials of *habeas corpus* and other basic American due process rights as they are being held, incomminicado, indefinitely.

Justice Davis began that crucial decision saying: "The importance of the main question presented by this record cannot be overstated; for it involves the very framework of the government and the principles of American liberty."

The dangerous importance of what has been done to American liberty since September 11, 2001, can also not be overstated—and must be resisted. It's worth repeating what Thomas Jefferson said: "The People are the only sure reliance for the preservation of our Liberty."

CHAPTER TWENTY-TWO

Spinning the Military Tribunal

> The American people will agree that [these rules for military tribunals] are a fair and balanced product that the American people can be proud of.
>
> —Victoria Clarke, Pentagon spokeswoman, CNN,
> March 22, 2002

> These concessions do little to change the structure of the tribunal as a makeshift court designed to produce predictable convictions.
>
> —Jonathan Turley, George Washington University law
> professor, *Los Angeles Times*, March 21, 2002

It took a while after 9/11, but concerning Bush's plan for military tribunals, choruses of dissent began to rise from bar associations, constitutional scholars, journalists, civil liberties groups, and citizens across the political spectrum.

Some of the sharpest criticism was directed at the initial, hastily and sweepingly drawn draft of the president's military order setting up the tribunals. The administration was surprised that the dissenters included members of the Washington legal establishment, as well as former military lawyers in the court-martial system. And *New York Times* columnist William Safire, a conservative, kept the drumbeat going on what he called "Bush's cockamamie order to deny the rule of law and public trial to those accused of terrorism."

The telegenic secretary of defense, Donald Rumsfeld, was put in charge of formulating the final regulations, and they have mollified some of the critics. The trials will be open, with the press in attendance. The evidence will have to show guilt beyond a reasonable doubt.

A sentence of capital punishment will require a unanimous verdict by the military court. And the defendant will not only get free military lawyers but can also hire a civilian attorney—if he can pay for one. Like most defendants on our death rows, however, many of the accused will be indigent.

The new regulations also provide for the presumption of innocence. But in an interview on *The NewsHour with Jim Lehrer* on PBS, Paul Wolfowitz, deputy secretary of defense, had a burst of candor. He said, "If anyone goes before this commission [as the tribunal is now called], it's because we have every reason to believe they have been involved in some of the most terrible crimes of this century."

It is not unreasonable to call this a presumption of guilt. Since there will be no appeals to our federal courts, and since the justice meted out is of a lesser standard than even that of courts-martial, the *New York Times*—in a March 22, 2002, lead editorial—was correct in saying that despite the improvements, "The tribunals would still constitute a separate, inferior system of justice, shielded from independent judicial review." And is it certain that only noncitizens will eventually be defendants?

Consider, moreover, the standards for the evidence that will be used to prove guilt beyond a reasonable doubt. Barbara Bradley, National Public Radio's first-rate reporter on our system of justice, gets to the core of this distortion of due process: "It'll be a lot easier to get evidence into these proceedings than, say, into a federal court or a military trial. Basically, the standard is any evidence that has 'probative value to a reasonable person' will be admitted, and that means hearsay or second-hand evidence could be admitted."

Hearsay includes rumors, gossip, and statements that cannot be verified. And the supposedly independent "reasonable persons" weighing which evidence can be admitted will be military officers chosen by their commander in chief, George W. Bush. He is the very person who decides, in the first place, who will be hauled before the military tribunal.

Jonathan Turley, the constitutional law professor at George Washington University I've often referred to, has served as a lawyer in national security cases in federal and military courts. In the *Los Ange-*

les Times (March 21, 2002), Turley emphasizes the distance between these tribunals and the American rule of law:

> It is clear that the new rules were written by prosecutors to govern their own prosecutions. The biggest changes are in areas that prosecutors find inconvenient, such as proving that evidence is authentic before using it. Accordingly, tribunal prosecutors will not have to "authenticate" evidence—or even show a chain of custody.

Where did the evidence come from originally? Whose hands did it pass through before being used against the defendant in a military tribunal? Could the so-called evidence have come from a person tortured by police in one of those countries where torture is a customary form of persuading prisoners to say what the authorities want to hear?

It is reasonable to expect that a prisoner convicted by the tribunal and sentenced to death, or to spend many of the rest of his years in prison, will want to appeal the verdict. Barbara Bradley explains his chances for due process (a quaint term in this context) both before the tribunal and during a subsequent appeal. The tribunal itself "will be composed of between three and seven military officers," she reports. "The presiding officer will have to be a JAG [judge advocate general] or a military lawyer, but the others don't have to have any legal training at all."

As for the board that will review the sentence, it will be composed of three or more military officers appointed by Secretary of Defense Rumsfeld. Rumsfeld can also temporarily include civilians—just like in the Old West, where the Dodge City sheriff could deputize "reasonable persons" to complete a posse.

Jonathan Turley makes the intriguing point that the review panel "*will not be permitted to apply the U.S. Constitution or federal law. This creates the mere pretense of legal process. . . .* The framers expressly denied the president the right to create and mete out his own form of justice. It takes more than a few rule changes to remove the 'kangaroo' from the court. One can shampoo and pedicure a kangaroo, but it does little to change the appearance of a president's own private menagerie of justice." (Emphasis added.)

Also, in these military tribunal rules is a section forbidding defense lawyers to talk to the press without first obtaining permission from the Justice Department. The language of this rule is broad, covering not only any classified information during the trial.

But much more offensive to the rule of American law, conversations between the defendants and their attorneys will be monitored by the government. This cuts to the core of the lawyer-client confidentiality that is essential to the Sixth Amendment right to effective counsel.

While these non-citizen defendants cannot claim rights under our Constitution, say the rules, it is very probable—in view of the Bush administration's treatment of American citizens designated as "enemy combatants"—that among the defendants in future military tribunals, there will be American citizens, shorn of their constitutional rights.

CHAPTER TWENTY-THREE

Vanishing Liberties

If Americans win a war (not just against Saddam Hussein but the longer-term struggle) and lose the Constitution, they will have lost everything.

—Lance Morrow, *Time*, March 10, 2003

On March 18, 2003, the Associated Press reported that at John Carroll University, in a Cleveland suburb, Justice Antonin Scalia said that "most of the rights you enjoy go way beyond what the Constitution requires" because "the Constitution just sets minimums." Accordingly, in wartime, Scalia emphasized, "the protections will be ratcheted down to the constitutional minimum."

I checked with the Supreme Court for a text of this ominous speech and was told Scalia didn't use a text that night, but the quotation appeared to be accurate.

I said, would Justice Scalia let me know? My question was relayed, but I've heard nothing since.

Most of the radical revisions of the Constitution that I and others have been writing about will ultimately be ruled on by the Supreme Court. Scalia indicates he will come down on the side of Bush and Ashcroft. A few days after the terrorist attacks on the World Trade Center and the Pentagon, Justice Sandra Day O'Connor said that as a result, we are "likely to experience more restrictions on our personal freedom than has ever been the case in our country."

In his book *All the Laws But One: Civil Liberties in Wartime* (Alfred A. Knopf, 1998), William Rehnquist, the chief justice of the United States, admiringly quoted Francis Biddle, Franklin D. Roosevelt's attorney general: "The Constitution has not greatly bothered any wartime president." And Rehnquist himself, who will be presiding over the constitutionality of the Bush-Ashcroft assaults on the Constitution, wrote in the same book, "In time of war, presidents may act in ways that push their legal authority to its outer limits, *if not beyond.*" (Emphasis added.) And writing of Lincoln's suspending *habeas corpus* during the Civil War, Rehnquist said, "It is difficult to quarrel with this decision."

Reacting to Rehnquist's deference to the executive branch in previous wars, Adam Cohen, legal affairs writer for the *New York Times*, wrote: "The people whose liberties are taken away are virtually invisible" in the pages of Rehnquist's book.

Meanwhile, in an invaluable new report by the Lawyers Committee for Human Rights, *Imbalance of Powers: How Changes to U.S. Law and Policy Since 9/11 Erode Human Rights and Civil Liberties* (March 2003; available by calling 212-845-5200), a section begins: "A mantle of secrecy continues to envelop the executive branch, largely with the acquiescence of Congress and the courts. [This] makes effective oversight impossible, upsetting the constitutional system of checks and balances."

So where is the oversight going to come from? If at all, first from the people pressuring Congress—provided enough of us know what is happening to our rights and liberties. And that requires, as James Madison said, a vigorous press, because the press has been "the beneficent source to which the United States owes much of the light which conducted [us] to the ranks of a free and independent nation."

But the media, with few exceptions, are failing to report consistently, and in depth, precisely how Bush and Ashcroft are undermining our fundamental individual liberties.

For example, in writing here about the Domestic Security Enhancement Act, the Justice Department's proposed sequel to the PATRIOT Act, I noted that it had been kept secret from Congress. A week before it was leaked by an understandably anonymous member of Ashcroft's staff, a representative of the Justice Department even lied to the Senate Judiciary Committee about its very existence.

A few sections in that chilling draft were briefly covered in some of the media. But these invasions of the Constitution were only a one- or two-day story in nearly all of the media.

How many Americans know that if the bill is passed (and Bush certainly won't veto it), they can be stripped of their citizenship if charged with giving "material support" to a group designated by the government as "terrorist"? Sending a check for the outfit's lawful activities—without knowing why it landed on Ashcroft's list—could make you a person without a country and put you behind bars here indefinitely.

How many Americans know that the FBI can get a warrant from the secret Foreign Intelligence Surveillance Court and go to a library or bookstore to find out what books you read or borrow if you are somehow, according to the FBI, connected to "terrorism"?

In the First Amendment Center's "Legal Watch" newsletter (March 11–17, 2003), Charles Haynes writes that "a warning sign greets patrons entering all ten of the county libraries in Santa Cruz, California." It says: "Beware, a record of the books you borrow may end up in the hands of the FBI. And if the FBI requests your records, librarians are prohibited by law from telling you about it." The message to the readers ends: "Questions about this policy should be directed to Attorney General John Ashcroft, Department of Justice, Washington, DC 20530."

Librarians—and bookstore owners—are also forbidden by this section of the law from telling the press of these visits by the FBI to inform John Ashcroft of what people on the list of suspects are reading.

More libraries around the country are warning their patrons to be cautious about which books they ask for. Shouldn't the press spread the news of this risk more widely?

And I've seen little in the media about a bill, "The Freedom to Read Protection Act of 2003," introduced in the House by Bernie Sanders (Independent, Vermont) that prevents the government from "searching for, or seizing from, a bookseller or library . . . materials that contain personally identifiable information concerning a patron of a bookseller or library." Under the bill, a higher standard than mere FBI suspicion will be required.

How many of you know the answer Assistant Attorney General Daniel J. Bryant sent Democratic Senator Patrick Leahy of Vermont about our expectation of privacy in bookstores and libraries?

"Any [such] right of privacy," says the Justice Department, "is necessarily and inherently limited since . . . the patron is reposing that information in the library or bookstore and assumes the risk that the entity may disclose it to another."

Have *you* ever assumed that the librarian or bookstore owner has a right to bypass your First Amendment right to read what you choose by telling "another" (the FBI) whether you read, for example, the *Village Voice*? Senator Leahy's office made that Justice Department letter available to the press. Have you seen it before now?

CHAPTER TWENTY-FOUR

Bush-Ashcroft vs. Homeland Security

Every time the administration removes another strand of the liberties in the Bill of Rights, we are told it has to be done in the vital interest of our homeland's security against the terrorists. But it is increasingly clear that we the citizens need to be secure from our government—not only where our liberties are concerned but also with regard to our health and our very lives.

An astonishing proposal in the Bush-Ashcroft draft of the Domestic Security Enhancement Act (DSEA), or "PATRIOT Act II"—hardly reported, if at all, in much of the press—subverts the Clean Air Act so radically that residents in towns and cities around the country could be affected.

I learned about this further obsession with secrecy by the administration from a very detailed analysis of the bill by Tim Edgar of the American Civil Liberties Union. He points out that the Clean Air Act requires that "corporations that use potentially dangerous chemicals must prepare an analysis of consequences of the release of such chemicals to the surrounding communities."

But under Section 202 of the DSEA, local residents will no longer have meaningful access to the analyses of the dangers to which they could be exposed. The information will be obtainable only in government reading rooms, Edgar adds, "in which copies could not be made and notes could not be taken."

But this material will not include "such basic information as 'the identity or location of any facility or any information from which the identity or location of the facility could be deduced.'"

It gets more bizarre. Only government officials will have full access to the analyses, including where these poisonous sites are, and thereby who owns them. But maybe somebody in such a facility, or in the government—like the anonymous member of Ashcroft's staff who leaked the draft of "Patriot II"—will feel compelled to leak this toxic information?

Forget it. Edgar notes that "government whistleblowers who reveal any information restricted under this section commit a criminal offense, even if their motivation was to protect the public from corporate wrongdoing or government neglect."

So where's the follow-up by the media? Will any of the elite Washington press corps ask the White House press secretary about the president's culpability if clueless citizens are hospitalized, or die, because of this government secrecy? Or, at one of the president's own rare press conferences, will a reporter demand whether the president plans to attend any of the resulting funerals?

Occasionally, a shard of information that can have an impact on the way we conduct our daily lives appears in the press. But again, where's the follow-up? In the March 15, 2003, New York *Daily News*, there was an Associated Press report from Washington that more than eighty FBI planes and helicopters are being used to "track and collect intelligence on suspected terrorists and other criminals." Note the key word, "suspected."

Among the FBI's aircraft, the AP story continues, "are several planes, known as Nightstalkers, equipped with infrared devices that allow agents to track people and vehicles in the dark.

"Other aircraft are outfitted with electronic surveillance equipment so agents can access listening devices placed in cars, in buildings, and even along streets, or listen to cell phone calls.... All fifty-six FBI field offices have access to aircraft.... [Legally,] no warrants are necessary for the FBI to track cars or people from the air." The good news, as it were, is that the FBI does need warrants to monitor cell phone calls, even if from a plane.

So where's the follow-up by the media?

A February 27, 2003, warning from the ACLU, about which I've seen few follow-ups in the press, begins: "A secretive new system for conducting background checks on all airline passengers threatens to create a bureaucratic machine for destroying Americans' privacy and a government blacklist that will harm innocent Americans."

Starting in March, the ACLU said, the Transportation Security Agency—which already has a "no-fly list" of people who might have some kind of connection with some kind of terrorist, or who have read the wrong books or magazines—has been testing the Computer Assisted Passenger Pre-Screening System (CAPPS II).

CAPPS II is a relative of retired Admiral John Poindexter's omnivorous data-mining Total Information Awareness program at the Defense Department, which—though suspended for a time by Congress—is very much alive as Poindexter perfects the equipment for tracking the patterns of your daily existence. Now called the Terrorism Information Awareness Program, it's the same extension of 1984.

There actually was a news conference at which the government proudly unveiled CAPPS II—anybody see any report of it in the press? According to the ACLU, "the government said that under the program Americans will be labeled as a 'green,' 'yellow,' or 'red' security risk. The red code would be reserved for those on terrorist watch lists," and they will be referred to law enforcement and grounded.

"Far less clear," the ACLU continues, "is who would get a yellow code in their file; those passengers would be subject to extra-intensive security screening."

Says the ACLU's Katie Corrigan: "This system threatens to create a permanent blacklisted underclass of Americans who cannot travel freely.... History suggests that the government will be capricious, unfair, and politically biased in deciding who to stamp as suspect. Anyone could get caught up in this system, with no way to get out."

There is no guarantee, says the ACLU, that a yellow code in a person's file would not be shared with "other government agencies at the federal, state, and local level, with intelligence agencies such as the CIA, and with foreign governments and international agencies—all of which could use those designations for many purposes, including employment decisions and the granting of government benefits."

If you were so designated, there is no procedure by which you'd be able to see what alleged information put you on the list. The government, says the ACLU, will not reveal the criteria for selection, or how—at the airport—you can challenge your being under suspicion. As the ACLU's Barry Steinhardt points out, "CAPPS II *won't be limited to air transportation for very long.* Nothing like it has ever been done in this country." (Emphasis added.)

Agreeing with the ACLU's alarm are the Christian Coalition, Phyllis Schlafly's Eagle Forum, the American Conservative Union, and People for the American Way. Where's the horde of Democrats running for the presidency?

CHAPTER TWENTY-FIVE

Conservatives Rise
for the Bill of Rights!

A significant development in the movement to resist the Ashcroft-Bush dismembering of the Bill of Rights is the growing coalition between conservative groups and such organizations as the American Civil Liberties Union and People for the American Way.

This has been going on—with only marginal attention from the media—since the ACLU organized a broad-based, though unsuccessful, fight to defeat the first USA PATRIOT Act toward the end of 2001. And it was the conservative Republican libertarian, Dick Armey, then majority leader in the House, who stripped the Orwellian Operation TIPS out of the Homeland Security Bill. Before retiring from Congress, Armey publicly accused the Justice Department of being "out of control" and "the most dangerous agency of government." That is more than most of the Democratic congressional leadership has ever said.

Moreover, from the beginning of Ashcroft's reign, a persistent critic has been Republican Bob Barr of Georgia, another conservative libertarian. Defeated in the last election, Barr is now a consultant for the ACLU.

On April 2, 2003, the ACLU sent a letter to Congress signed by sixty-seven liberal and conservative organizations—ranging from People for the American Way and the American Library Association to Gun Owners of America and Americans for Tax Reform. The head of the latter is Grover Norquist, who has frequent access to the upper echelons of the White House. Also on board in that letter was the influential American Conservative Union. At the invitation of its president, David Keene, I spoke about Ashcroft's raids on the Constitution at the annual Conservative Union Political Action Conference earlier this year. It was the first time in *Village Voice* history that someone from the paper appeared at that gathering.

Then, on April 10, 2003, the ACLU hosted a forum called "Discussion with Conservatives: State of Civil Liberties Post 9/11," at which prominent conservative organizations joined publicly with groups from the Left for the first time.

Laura Murphy, director of the ACLU's Washington legislative office, set the agenda: "Congress must reconsider some of the measures that were adopted with little debate in the weeks after the terrorist attacks. We are unanimous in our strong belief that Congress must treat with deep skepticism any additional requests for new intelligence-gathering powers."

She was referring, of course, to the startling revision of the Bill of Rights in Ashcroft's draft of the DSEA. Scornfully, Bob Barr calls it "Son of Patriot." (For details of that draft, see chapter 18, "Red Alert for the Bill of Rights.")

In the April 15 *Dallas Morning News*, Michelle Mittelstadt, who covered the April 10 coalition forum assembled by the ACLU, quoted Mark Corallo, a Justice Department spokesman, as saying that "Patriot Act II" will be sent to Congress later this year. In the draft are provisions for secret arrests and stripping Americans of citizenship for "support" of organizations whose "terrorist" activities are unknown to those who send checks.

I would have thought that this public conjunction in Washington of leading right and left organizations was of sufficient news interest to at least get C-SPAN to cover it. But there was no television coverage at all, and only a few newspaper articles.

The tone of the meeting was reflected in a comment by Lori Waters, executive director of Phyllis Schlafly's very conservative Eagle Forum. She was quoted by Jake Tapper in his valuable, extensive report on the coalition session in the April 11 *Salon*. At the beginning of her remarks, Waters said, "Everyone in this room is a suspect until it's proven that you're not."

Circulating around the room was the news that Republican Senator Orrin Hatch of Utah had introduced an amendment that would make every section of the first USA PATRIOT Act permanent. That legislation included a "sunset clause" that required Congress to decide in December 2005 whether the act is too far-reaching to be renewed.

(Hatch has since, for the time being, withdrawn that amendment.) It was because of that sunset clause that some apprehensive members of Congress—notably the late Senator Paul Wellstone, Democrat from Minnesota—gingerly voted for the PATRIOT Act.

Said Grover Norquist of Americans for Tax Reform at the April 10 ACLU session, "I would support legislation that would sunset all legislation passed during a time of war. And I would vote against any legislation somebody felt they had to name 'Patriot.' [Which no one would have felt the need to do] if it were a worthwhile bill. [That name] was used to mau-mau people because it looks bad on a thirty-second commercial to have voted against it." Gee, that line could have been in the *Village Voice.*

As Jake Tapper reported, David Keene of the Conservative Union, remembering how Ashcroft so swiftly pushed the PATRIOT Act through Congress, said, "I don't know that 5 percent of the people who voted for that bill ever read it."

At a press conference after the April 10 meeting, Bob Barr was asked how he and his bipartisan colleagues expected to counter the large public support for the Bush-Ashcroft promises of security in return for giving up individual liberties. "People need to learn," Barr said, "that we're all subject to having our privacy invaded. . . . These laws will dramatically change the way we go about conducting our society."

They already have, as these conservatives, including Barr, well know. Norquist, explaining his presence at an ACLU-sponsored gathering, told *Salon* that previously he'd thought the ACLU and liberals would take care of threats to the Constitution. But, he said to the *Dallas Morning News* (April 13, 2003), "I'm not sure given the Republican control of the House and the Senate and the government that we can count on our left-of-center friends to look out for some of these issues."

Especially since most of the congressional Democratic leadership has not been paying attention to diminishing constitutional rights. Grover Norquist told Jake Tapper that in his meetings "with friends in the White House," he brings up the attacks on civil liberties "quite a bit" as "one of the top issues." But Norquist's impact will not be on the uneducable Bush and Ashcroft, but rather on his fellow conservatives in and out of Congress. On both sides of the aisle, there is rising displeasure with John Ashcroft's stewardship of the Constitution. But in April 2003, he moved to insulate himself even further from Congress.

CHAPTER TWENTY-SIX

Protecting John Ashcroft
from Congress—and Us

No other national administration, in my more than forty years of covering the state of the Constitution's health, has more persistently protected itself from scrutiny—and public oversight—than George W. Bush's executive branch and, particularly, his Justice Department.

It was only after an understandably anonymous whistleblower in the Justice Department leaked the draft of John Ashcroft's proposed Domestic Security Enhancement Act that Congress—and the rest of the citizenry—learned about plans to specifically authorize secret arrests for the first time in our history; collect and maintain DNA samples of anyone "suspected" of some kind of association with designated terrorist groups; and strip Americans of citizenship for "supporting" such groups, even if they had no idea of their "terrorist" bent.

Three days after the leak, as I've noted, Senator Patrick Leahy of Vermont, ranking Democratic member of the Judiciary Committee, said: "For months, and as recently as just last week, Justice Department officials have denied to members of the Judiciary Committee that they were drafting another antiterrorism package."

On both sides of the congressional aisle, there is resentment of this secrecy in the imperious Justice Department. Despite this, Ashcroft is trying to further insulate himself.

In April 2003, the Justice Department's Office of Legislative Affairs has, by order of the attorney general, instructed all members of the Justice Department to inform that office "ahead of time and as soon as possible" before they participate in any briefings on Capitol Hill or engage in "substantive conversations" with members of Congress or their staff on Capitol Hill.

Every Justice Department employee is to be tracked to make sure—said the directive—"that the Department speaks with one voice on Capitol Hill . . . Please let us know when you receive a phone call from, or plan to place a call to, House and Senate staff and Members of Congress.

"Moreover," the trackers add, "in almost all cases . . . we will accompany you to briefings." (In Iraq before the war, this form of government supervision was exercised by "minders.")

Said Senator Patrick Leahy, "If this [tracking] was to facilitate answers to Congress, that would be one thing, but the administration's overwhelming impulse has been to limit the flow of information, and that has made congressional oversight of this Justice Department a never-ending ordeal."

Republican Senator Charles Grassley of Iowa called the directive "an attempt to muzzle whistleblowers," saying on *Fox News*, "We are all working for the American people to have maximum communication among the branches of government. This is an attempt to control information. We want to make sure that what we pass in Congress works the way we wanted it to, and that the money is spent the way we intended. We need a maximum flow of information to make the separation of powers work."

Can you imagine what would happen to a member of the Justice Department who—on seeing particularly radical revisions of the Bill of Rights in a draft of a possible "Patriot Act III"—tells the Justice Department's Office of Legal Affairs that he or she, in conscience, feels bound to tell Congress of this Ashcroft plan?

The tracking memorandum is all the more reason for Congress to act on at least the Leahy-Grassley FBI Reform Act to protect not only FBI agents in the Justice Department, but all the other Justice employees, from retaliation when they consider it essential for Congress to exercise its constitutional right to oversee the department.

Among the reforms in the Leahy-Grassley act is the strengthening of whistleblower protections for FBI employees. Leahy points out that "the FBI is currently exempted from the Whistleblower Protection Act, and its employees are only protected by internal Department of Justice regulations."

For example, when Minneapolis Field Office Agent Coleen Rowley wrote her whistleblowing letter and then testified famously in the June 6, 2002, Judiciary Committee Oversight Hearing, she was not protected under current FBI regulations, and she certainly did not inform the Justice Department before her whistleblowing letter.

I hope Leahy and Grassley are not the only members of Congress who reject the Ashcroft rule that any member of the Justice Department must be accompanied by a "minder" when communicating with members of Congress or their staff—as well as having to get permission to even go to Capitol Hill.

As constitutional law professor Jonathan Turley has noted (*Los Angeles Times*, January 2, 2003), in the Bush administration's "campaign for greater government powers, the Constitution (and its separation of powers) are increasingly cited as exposing the nation to risks . . . (Since 9/11) the Constitution has gone from an objective to be satisfied to an obstacle to national defense . . . As these changes mount, at what point do we become something other than a free and democratic nation . . . It is unclear when this 'war on terror' will end. But if it does end and we win, what will we be other than victorious?"

CHAPTER TWENTY-SEVEN

Will American Liberty Survive the War on Terrorism?

As a culture, our tolerance for fear is low, and our capacity to do something about it is unrivaled. We could have the highest degree of public safety the world has ever seen. But what would that country look like, and what will it be like to live in it?

—Matthew Brezinski, "Fortress America,"
New York Times Magazine, February 23, 2002

In an editorial on citizen Yaser Hamdi—imprisoned indefinitely without charges and without being able to see his lawyer, or anyone else except his guards, in a Navy brig on American soil—the *Washington Post* expressed shock:

> To yank an American out of the court system and then maintain, purely on the government's word, that he is not entitled to challenge the evidence against him, is a breathtakingly radical act . . . Among the many confrontations between civil liberties and the war on terror, the government is advancing no contention more dangerous.

As I've shown in this book, the government—with little resistance from congressional Democrats or Republicans—continues to advance even more dangerous contentions. But citizen resistance to these radical assaults on the Bill of Rights is also continuing. On February 10, 2003, the American Bar Association, the nation's largest organization of lawyers, overwhelmingly called for a fundamental change in the government's imprisonment of what it calls "enemy combatants"—such as Yaser Hamdi.

Insisting that these American citizens be given access to lawyers as well as *meaningful* judicial review of their confinement, Neal Sonnett, head of the ABA's task force on enemy combatants, said that at stake is the very principle of due process—fairness—that is the core of our system of justice.

The ABA House of Delegates declared: "We are a great nation not just because we are the most powerful, but because we are the most democratic. But indefinite detention, denial of counsel, and overly secret proceedings could tear at the Bill of Rights, the very fabric of our great democracy. We must ensure that we do not erode our cherished constitutional safeguards and that we strengthen the rule of law . . . We must get this right. The people of this great country deserve no less."

It is also up to the media—the free and independent press—to make clear to Americans that, as UCLA law professor Erwin Chemerinsky emphasizes in the *Los Angeles Daily Journal,*

> There is no precedent for the Bush administration's claim of authority. No Supreme Court case, and for that matter no case of any court in the United States, ever has upheld the government's authority to detain a person indefinitely without complying with the Constitution by labeling the individual an enemy combatant.

We are in clear danger of becoming a country in which, as Anthony Lewis—twice a *New York Times* Pulitzer Prize winner for illuminating the Constitution—writes, "the government can impose solitary confinement, perhaps for life, if it simply avoids giving a prisoner a trial."

Lewis asks what would "the average American" think if told that he or she "could be taken off the street and imprisoned forever without being able to call a lawyer?"

What we are all faced with is an administration that only believes in the rule of law if it can continue to change the rule of law in the shifting name of national security.

Defense Secretary Donald Rumsfeld, for example, said directly and chillingly (*Newsday*, September 15, 2002): "Anything that comes up in the United States tends to be looked at as a law enforcement matter . . . 'decide whether or not he's guilty or innocent and give him due process.' Of course if . . . you've got the risk of terrorists . . . killing thousands or tens of thousands of people, you're not terribly interested in whether or not the person is potentially a subject for law enforcement." You're not terribly interested in the American system of justice.

And so, a person can be held indefinitely, shorn of due process, or—as indicated in my previous chapters on the torturing of prisoners or the official designated killers of suspected terrorists—the person can be killed without any recourse to the rule of law.

Or, it's worth repeating, as Assistant Attorney General Michael Chertoff said, when he was head of the Justice Department's criminal division: "When we are talking about preventing acts of war against us, the judicial model doesn't work."

As for this administration's omnivorous mandating of secrecy in so many of its restrictions of fundamental liberties, professor Stephen Schulhofer of New York University Law School emphasizes in *The American Prospect* (March 2003):

> Secrecy across the board, without any obligation to present case-specific reasons for it in court, has less to do with the war on terrorism than with the administration's consistent efforts, firmly in place before 9/11, to insulate executive action from public scrutiny.
>
> The cumulative effect of these efforts is an unprecedented degree of power—an attempt simultaneously to cut off the right to counsel or judicial review, and any ability of the press to report what happens to individuals arrested on U.S. soil.

Or, as the *Washington Post* warned in a December 31, 2002, editorial:

> The broad danger . . . is that a kind of alternative legal

system has come into existence for an ill-defined category of offenses involving national security . . . The environment they create cumulatively is troubling. This is particularly true because *the war they are intended for may prove a near-permanent state of affairs, and victory may be difficult to recognize.*

It is an environment in which the president has nearly unbridled authority to pick the legal regime most advantageous at every step of an investigation, or a proceeding against an individual—in which a person can be plucked out of the protections of the Bill of Rights at the whim of the executive branch of government . . . That's a dangerous prospect for civil liberties, and in the long run, for effective counterterrorism as well. (Emphasis added).

Another perspective of what can be the future of this nation, under a shadow Constitution, could be found in a February 22, 2003, story in the *New York Times* about a journalist in Iran who has been working, at his peril, for a dependable rule of constitutional law in that country.

Mashallah Shamsolvaezin, a political prisoner for nineteen months for "harming Islam" in his writings, said of the absence of basic guarantees of due process in Iran's system of justice, "There's a minefield in front of us, and we don't have the map. In democracies, the people have access to the map of the minefields. But here, the government keeps the map secret. It wants to keep changing it whenever it wants."

In this country, the map of the minefields to liberty—and freedom—keeps changing, and We the People have less and less access to it. And to the Bill of Rights.

Soon after September 11, 2001, Supreme Court Justice Anthony Kennedy visited a number of high schools in order to regenerate students' knowledge of fundamental American values. At Stuyvesant High School in New York City, he warned the students that the terrorist attacks showed ominously that "democracy may be stolen."

As is becoming increasingly evident, not only the terrorists can steal democracy. And that's why, speaking of the government's sweeping use of the term "enemy combatants," the *Washington Post* warned us all on March 28, 2003, that "An unbridled power of military detention will not forever be deployed only against would-be terrorists."

CHAPTER TWENTY-EIGHT

Dick Armey's Farewell Address

On December 6, 2002, retiring House Majority Leader Dick Armey gave his farewell address at the National Press Club in Washington. I wish it had been on prime-time television.

The conservative Republican warned us all that, in the war to preserve our freedoms against terrorism, we must guard against the "awful dangerous seduction of sacrificing our freedoms for safety against this insidious threat that comes right into our neighborhoods."

Armey emphasized that "we the people had better keep an eye on ... our government. Not out of contempt or lack of appreciation or disrespect, but out of a sense of guardianship.

"How do you use these tools we have given you to make us safe in such a manner that'll preserve our freedom? ... Freedom is no policy for the timid. And my plaintive plea to all my colleagues that remain in this government as I leave it is, for our sake, for my sake, for heaven's sake, don't give up on freedom!"

Hearing Armey's speech, I was again reminded of one of the last conversations I had with the late Supreme Court Justice William Brennan. He and Armey greatly disagreed on some issues, but not on certain essential sections of the Bill of Rights.

"Look, pal," Justice Brennan told me, "we've always known—the Framers knew—that liberty is a fragile thing."

Libertarian conservative Bob Barr is working with the ACLU on privacy and other civil liberties issues. Not surprisingly, some politically correct members of the ACLU are disturbed.

In a letter to the membership, Executive Director Anthony Romero reminded them that "throughout our eighty-two-year-old history, we have aligned ourselves with people who can help us protect civil liberties regardless of their political party. ... The Civil Rights Act of 1991, signed into law by President George H. W. Bush, was the result of . . . unlikely allies across the Democratic and Republican parties."

Romero adds that the ACLU "has no permanent friends and no permanent enemies, just permanent values." Illustrating that point is Illinois Republican Congressman Henry Hyde, who has often clashed with the ACLU. But he has worked with it to protect free speech on college campuses and to limit the right of government to seek defendants' assets in certain cases. "They are," he says of the ACLU, "a very useful and productive force in jurisprudence."

As Armey and Barr have warned, the continuing invasions of basic liberties in the USA PATRIOT Act and the subsequent insistence by the administration on setting up an additional parallel legal system affect all of our freedoms. And the ACLU has proved essential in that battle. For more and more Americans, it is no longer an epithet to refer to "card-carrying members of the ACLU." And hundreds of thousands are joining the rapidly growing number of the Bill of Rights Defense Committees in towns and cities across the country.

As Dick Armey says: "Don't give up on freedom!"

CHAPTER TWENTY-NINE

Knowing Enough of Our History to Save Our Future

I know of no safe repository of the ultimate powers of our society but the people themselves; and if we think them not enlightened enough to exercise their control with a wholesome discretion, the remedy is not to take it from them, but to inform their discretion by education.

—Thomas Jefferson

The extent to which many Americans need to know the history of this nation to be moved to join the resistance to the government's dismembering their constitutional liberties was revealed in the First Amendment Center's *State of the First Amendment* 2002. This is an annual survey by the Center, based at Vanderbilt University in Nashville, and conducted with the University of Connecticut's Center for Survey Research and Analysis.

In the five-year history of the survey, this—said Kenneth Paulson, executive director of the First Amendment Center—was the first time "almost half of those surveyed said that the First Amendment goes too far in the rights it guarantees. About 49 percent said the First Amendment gives us too much freedom . . .

"The least popular First Amendment right is freedom of the press. For example, 42 percent of respondents said the press in America has too much freedom to do what it wants, roughly the same as the 2001 survey"—which was taken before the 9/11 terrorist attacks.

In a more encouraging response, about 40 percent said that they have "too little access to information about the war on terrorism, compared with 16 percent who said there's too much. And 48 percent said there's too little access to government records, compared to 8 percent who said there's too much."

Most disturbing in the survey were the answers to this question: "Can you name any of the specific rights that are guaranteed by the First Amendment?" Only 14 percent knew that the First Amendment specifically guarantees freedom of the press. But 58 percent are aware that freedom of speech is part of that fundamental right. However, only 18 percent cited freedom of religion as a First Amendment guarantee; and just 2 percent knew that all of us have the right "to petition the Government for a redress of grievances"—such grievances as serial violations of the Bill of Rights.

"This is a living Constitution," said John Marshall, chief justice of the Supreme Court from 1801 to 1835. But, as current Justice Anthony Kennedy warns, "The Constitution needs renewal and understanding each generation, or else it's not going to last."

To understand the Constitution requires knowledge of the serious threats to its core guarantees throughout American history. In the October 2002 issue of *American Heritage*, Frank J. Williams, chief justice of the Supreme Court of Rhode Island, emphasized that "War and its effect on civil liberties remain a frightening unknown."

To sharpen that point, he added more details than in my previous chapter in this book on what the revered Abraham Lincoln did to the Constitution during the Civil War. He not only suspended *habeas corpus*—as George W. Bush has, with regard to American citizens held without charges in this country as "enemy combatants"—but, says Justice Williams, quoting historian Jay Winick's article "Security Comes Before Liberty" in the *Wall Street Journal* (October 23, 2001), "Lincoln subjected all persons discouraging volunteer enlistments to martial law. To enforce this decree, a network of provost marshals promptly imprisoned several hundred antiwar activists and draft resisters, journalists, and prominent civic leaders." Many were tried by military tribunals.

Justice Williams adds that "it appears the Bush administration is confounded on the use of military tribunals," and therefore, we ought to keep in mind what Judge Mark Neely wrote in the epilogue to his book, *The Fate of Liberty: Abraham Lincoln and Civil Liberties* (Oxford University Press, 1991) : "The clearest lesson is that there is no clear lesson in the Civil War—no neat precedents, no ground rules, no maps. War and its effect on civil liberties remain a frightening unknown."

But there is a clear and essential rule of law that resulted from that war—the 1866 decision by the United States Supreme Court in the *Milligan* case that I have quoted at length. Abraham Lincoln, the court ruled, was a serial violator of the Constitution during the Civil War while the civilian courts were open.

Americans need to remember that period in our history when the president recognized no limit to his powers. And in that tradition during the war against terrorism, George W. Bush and his attorney general have been telling the courts that they must defer to the president's overweening authority over the Constitution.

In the Civil War, the courts waited too long to restore the Constitution. Will the present Supreme Court protect the Constitution during the limitless war against terrorism?

On July 13, 2002, in a lead editorial, the *Washington Post* focused on the Bush administration's doctrine of judicial submission to the executive branch:

> FBI Director Robert Mueller has said that a sizable number of people in this country are associated with terrorist groups, yet have so far done nothing wrong [so] there is no basis to indict them.
>
> How many of them, one wonders, [might the government, bypassing the Court] hold as enemy combatants? And how many of them would later turn out to be something else entirely?

And how much later would they be released?

CHAPTER THIRTY

A Secret Meeting in 1773 on Which "The Political Salvation of America Depends"

In an April 11, 2003, speech at the University of Mississippi in Oxford, Supreme Court Justice Antonin Scalia once again declared himself an "originalist" or "textualist" in the way he interprets the Constitution. To make sure he is always aware of what the Framers precisely meant when they wrote the Constitution, Justice Scalia said proudly that he uses an eighteenth-century dictionary to guide his decisions on the Supreme Court.

Justice Scalia would have a deeper understanding of why—*because* of the "living document" that is the Constitution—we are Americans, if he paid more attention to the actual history in that century of how we came to have the Revolution that produced the Constitution.

On March 12, 1773, in a secret meeting in the Apollo Room of the Raleigh Tavern in Williamsburg, Virginia—where the House of Burgesses was assembled—Thomas Jefferson, Patrick Henry, Richard Henry Lee, and others of their colleagues decided that "urgent steps must be taken if they [and all Americans] were to become a free and independent people."

In Boston, the Sons of Liberty (Sam Adams among them) had started a local Committee of Correspondence on November 2, 1772, to spread the news throughout the colonies of British invasions of Americans' free-born rights. Within three months, there were many more such committees in Massachusetts alone. At the meeting in the Raleigh Tavern, the Virginians, beginning to create an independent nation, formed the first Committee of Correspondence in that state.

As Norine Dickson Campbell wrote in *Patrick Henry: Patriot and Statesman* (Devin Adair, 1969), Jefferson, in a memoir, recalled, "We were all sensible that the most urgent of all measures was that of coming to an understanding with all the colonies to consider . . . a common cause to all, and to produce a unity of action.

"For this purpose," Jefferson continued, "a committee of correspondence in each colony would be the best instrument for intercommunication."

On April 4, 1773, Richard Henry Lee wrote John Dickinson (both were later to be delegates to the 1787 Constitutional Convention) that this interconnection between the colonies would be the union "on which the political salvation of America depends."

The Committees of Correspondence—brought to life again for the political salvation of America in today's Bill of Rights Defense Committees—led back then to the Continental Congress, which, in its second meeting, adopted a resolution on July 2, 1776, that "these united Colonies are, and of right ought to be, free and independent states." Two days later, the Declaration of Independence was adopted.

On April 21, 2003, on the front page of the *Washington Post*, Evelyn Nieves reported a new declaration of independence in Arcata, California, a town 279 miles north of San Francisco. It had become the first city or town in the country to pass an ordinance requiring the nine managers of the city—including the city manager, the city attorney, and the city police chief—to refuse to *voluntarily* "cooperate with investigations, interrogations, or arrest procedures, public or clandestine"—from outside law enforcement agencies—that could violate the Constitution, and particularly, its Bill of Rights.

The ordinance is aimed directly at the USA PATRIOT Act and other orders by the attorney general, the FBI, and other government law-enforcement and intelligence agencies.

This official defiance of the national government by most of the sixteen thousand citizens of Arcata, who intensely believe their fundamental liberties are being violated, was preceded by resolutions condemning the USA PATRIOT Act in towns and cities across the country.

As I've indicated previously, this is a movement started and largely directed by the original Bill of Rights Defense Committee in Northampton, Massachusetts. But those protest resolutions were without the force of law. An ordinance, however, is a local or state statute or regulation.

The ordinance was written by City Council member David Meserve, a builder and contractor in his fifties. I asked him if the police chief or other city officials had objected to what Meserve calls "a nonviolent preemptive attack" on the Federal government's revision of the Bill of Rights.

"In the room while I was writing the ordinance," Meserve told me, "were City Attorney Nancy Diamond, City Manager Dan Hauser, and Interim Police Chief Randy Mendosa." All were in favor of sending this message to John Ashcroft and the members of Congress from that area.

Among the provisions of the "Defending Civil Rights and Liberties" addition to Arcata's municipal code is that management employees of the city must notify the city manager when

> contacted by another law enforcement agency and asked to cooperate or assist with an investigation, interrogation, or arrest procedure under provisions of the USA PATRIOT Act (Public Law 107-56), Homeland Security Act (Public Law 107-296), or related executive orders, or future enacted law, executive order, or regulation, when such procedure is in violation of an individual's civil rights or civil liberties as specified in the Bill of Rights and Fourteenth Amendment of the United States Constitution.

However, in addition to notifying the city manager that such forces hostile to American liberties have come to the city, another part of the ordinance makes possible a *High Noon* confrontation between Federal agents and local town officials on the streets of Arcata.

The key word in the ordinance is "voluntarily" (shall not "voluntarily" cooperate with investigations that could violate the rights of Arcata's residents.)

Therefore, if an Arcata management official is ordered to give information about a resident and is threatened with legal action for refusing the information to the FBI that could lead to a court test of the ordinance. Can a city pass a law defying the federal government? Arcata would surely get free legal help from the American Civil Liberties Union, and, as Councilwoman Connie Stewart cheerfully says, "The Quakers would definitely hold a bake sale." Actually, the official would have to obey the court's decision if it went against him or her.

The reason, of course, for this official statutory challenge to the president and John Ashcroft by a small city is that it symbolizes a significant and continually growing national grassroots opposition to the administration's war on the Bill of Rights as it combats terrorism. The message is: Attention must be paid!

In covering the story of the first city ordinance, the Sunday *San Francisco Chronicle* noted on April 19 that the eighty-three previous resolutions "condemning the PATRIOT Act" at the time ranged from San Francisco itself, Berkeley, and Oakland, California, to Baltimore and Detroit, while Mill Valley, California, "joined the list just last Monday."

And the front-page *Washington Post* account of this enthusiastic disrespect of John Ashcroft noted that "In Hawaii, home to many Japanese-Americans who vividly recall the Japanese internment camps of World War II, Democratic State Representative Roy Takumi introduced a resolution on the Patriot Act as a way to raise debate," which is what Arcata has done.

The resolution in Hawaii may be seen as symbolic, Takumi said, but he expects that as "a number of states begin to pass similar resolutions," then Congress will "realize our concerns. I hope to see that what we've done here plays a role in mobilizing people to take action" around the country.

And the April 21, 2003, *Washington Post* story used the Arcata ordinance to link to the fact that "Lawmakers and lobbyists on both sides of the political spectrum are beginning to sound alarms about the antiterrorism act" and the "unprecedented powers" it gives the government.

In Arcata, the *San Francisco Chronicle* reported that Susan Mattson "said as she rang up customers at her Garden Gate gift shop overlooking the rustic little town square, 'I don't know anyone in town who likes the PATRIOT Act.'"

CHAPTER THIRTY-ONE

The Chilling Effect
on Our Freedoms

During the fierce debates in the new America on whether the Constitution, written in 1787, should be ratified, there was fear among the dissenters that a national federal government would be too powerful. During that debate, the proposed Constitution, which did not yet have a Bill of Rights, was attacked by Robert Yates, writing under the pseudonym "Brutus."

In Bernard Bailyn's *To Begin the World Anew* (Knopf, 2003), Brutus, much concerned with the new government's power to tax, predicted that this federal government "will introduce itself into every corner of the city and country. It [the national government] will wait upon the ladies at their toilet, and will not leave them in any of their domestic concerns; it will accompany them to the ball, the play, the assembly . . . it will enter the house of every gentleman . . . it will take cognizance of the professional man in his office, or his study . . . it will follow the mechanic to his shop, and in his work, and will haunt him in his family, in his bed . . . it will penetrate into the most obscure cottage; and finally, it will light upon the head of every person in the United States."

It was as if "Brutus" could have foreseen beyond the power to tax, Admiral John Poindexter's Terrorism Information Awareness System in the Pentagon, or the ever increasing electronic surveillance of the citizenry by John Ashcroft. Soon after the hasty passage of the USA PATRIOT Act in the immediate wake of 9/11, Mindy Tucker, then the spokesperson for the Justice Department, promised: "This is just the first step. There will be additional items to come." In the preceding chapters, you have seen many of these items in Brutus's vision, and so much more.

In the April 11, 2003, issue of *The Chronicle of Higher Education*, the authoritative source of news and analysis concerning college and university affairs, Judith Grant, an associate professor of political science and women's studies at the University of Southern California, wrote in an article titled "Uncle Sam Over My Shoulder":

> I am now experiencing what American legal scholars call 'a chilling effect,' and I was indeed aware of it as a sort of chill running up my spine—a half-second of anxiety, almost subconscious, the moment I heard that the [USA PATRIOT] Act had been passed.
>
> I feel that chill again when I realize that I now pause a moment before I write almost anything. I think about how a government official might read my writing if he or she were trying to build a (completely unjustified) case against me. I worried even while I wrote that last sentence, then I worried about my worry. Might someone in the Justice Department ask: "Why would she be worried if she were doing nothing wrong?"

In the April 20, 2003, Letters section of the *New York Times*, Tina Rosan of Cambridge, Massachusetts, comments on a previous *Times* story, "Muslims Hesitating on Gifts as U.S. Scrutinizes Charities":

> Of course Muslims in the United States are "hesitating" to give money to charities because they are afraid . . . Many have been detained without trial. Given this environment, Muslims are trying to stay under the radar. They don't want a contribution to a charity to put them on a suspect list or cause them to end up in jail. Unfortunately the news media have not been paying attention to the severe violation of civil liberties at home. The real truth is much deeper and darker.

In the April 21, 2003, *Newsday*, columnist Sheryl McCarthy told of a twenty-six-year-old mechanical engineer, Daniel Ueda, and twenty-eight-year-old Carey Larsen, who were arrested in a demonstration "outside the offices of The Carlyle Group, a private investment house with holdings in the defense industry":

> At police headquarters both Ueda and Larsen were asked questions that seemed strange, considering the minor offenses with which they were charged. Questions like: how many protests had they participated in, what groups were they affiliated with, how they heard about the demonstrations . . . how they felt about the war with Iraq and whether they thought the United States should have entered World War II. Yes, really.
>
> When they balked at answering the political questions, they were warned they'd be held longer if they didn't cooperate.

When *New York Times* columnist Joyce Purnick (April 21) asked the New York City Police Department if the information obtained from such questioning could be used to infiltrate political groups, the Police Department's chief spokesman, Michael O'Looney, said: "I'm going to leave it with that." He refused to answer the question that brought back my memories of the days of J. Edgar Hoover's COIN-TELPRO, when the FBI, at will, infiltrated and disrupted entirely lawful groups.

Donna Lieberman, executive director of the New York Civil Liberties Union, is aware of the history of COINTELPRO, and she told Joyce Purnick: "When people are asked about their political affiliations, it's intimidation. It's discouraging people from exercising their fundamental right to criticize government."

So when Judith Grant feels "a chilling effect" when she writes for *The Chronicle of Higher Education*, she may not be entirely without reason to be somewhat intimidated by the environment that John Ashcroft has created.

Sam Adams, the eighteenth-century patriot, once said of this new sweet land of liberty: "Driven from every other corner of the earth, freedom of thought and the right of private judgement in matters of conscience, direct their course to this happy country as their last asylum."

Like "Brutus," Sam Adams did not foresee the Bush-Ashcroft omnivorous surveillance of the residents of this "last asylum."

Sam Adams was overly sanguine about the future of freedom of conscience here. In 1858, Abraham Lincoln, speaking in Edwardsville, Illinois—before assuming the powers of the presidency—spoke to a truth that George W. Bush would do well to keep in mind:

> What constitutes the bulwark of our own liberty and independence? It is not our frowning battlements, our bristling seacoasts, our army and navy. These are not our reliance against tyranny . . . Our reliance is the love of liberty . . . Destroy this spirit and you have planted the seeds of despotism at your door.

This was the same Abraham Lincoln who suspended *habeas corpus*, imprisoned many Americans who dissented from his policies, and set up military tribunals to dispose of citizens of contrary views—even though the civilian courts were still open.

Then there was Franklin Delano Roosevelt, who earnestly told the nation:

> We must scrupulously guard the civil liberties of all citizens, whatever their background. We must remember that any oppression, any injustice, any hatred, is a wedge designed to attack our civilization.

It was the same Franklin Delano Roosevelt who signed Executive Order No. 9066 that sent Japanese-Americans into detention camps, which they rightly regarded as concentration camps.

When, in August 2002, Federal Judge Damon J. Keith, writing for the Sixth Circuit Court of Appeals, ruled against the Bush administration's closing of all deportation hearings to the press and the public, though the Third Circuit voted the other way, he emphasized:

> Democracies die behind closed doors. The only safe-

guard on this extraordinary government power is in the public, deputizing the press as the guardians of their liberty. An informed public is the most potent of all restraints on government . . . the First Amendment, through a free press, protects the people's right to know that their government acts fairly, lawfully, and accurately.

But veteran journalist Jack Nelson, retired Washington bureau chief of the *Los Angeles Times*, told a First Amendment Center conference on March 12, 2003:

President Bush has gone beyond just being extremely secretive about the conduct of the government's business. In the name of fighting terrorism, he has amassed powers and wrapped them in a cloak of resilience to normal oversight by Congress and the judiciary. *No president since I've been a reporter has so tried to change the very structure of government to foster secrecy.* (Emphasis added.)

Even the Fourth Circuit Court of Appeals—the most conservative Federal appellate court in the country—rebuked the Bush administration in the case of Zacarias Moussaoui, accused of involvement in a terrorist conspiracy. Reported the April 2, 2003, *Washington Post*:

The court chided the government for "simultaneously prosecuting the defendant and attempting to restrict his ability to use information [in court] that he feels is necessary to defend himself against the prosecution . . .

Courts must not be remiss in protecting a defendant's right to a full and meaningful presentation of his claim to innocence."

Concerning this case, Donald Rehkopf, chairman of the Military Law Committee of the National Association of Criminal Defense Lawyers, accused the government of "inventing the law as they go along. The Constitution," he reminded the administration—echoing the Supreme Court in the 1866 *Milligan* case—"is not suspended, even during time of war."

And when the government proposed, in "Patriot Act II," to strip Americans of their citizenship if they give "support" to an organization cited by the administration as implicated in terrorism—even if the accused American is unaware of that part of the group's activities—human rights attorney Joanne Mariner noted in an article on www.findlaw.com ("Patriot II's Attack on Citizenship", March 3, 2003) how Ashcroft and Bush also invent the law in proposing to take away the most essential of all American rights, our citizenship. Professor Mariner wrote:

> If you help fund an orphanage administered by one of the three Chechen separatist groups that the government has labeled as terrorist, or if you give pharmaceutical supplies to a medical outpost run by the East Turkestan Islamic Movement, or if you are on the wrong side of any of a number of other political conflicts in the world, you are vulnerable to the loss of your citizenship.

Although you "would be able to challenge this determination in court," she continued, you would "not necessarily succeed." Particularly, if during the limitless war on terrorism, our courts keep deferring to the government, bypassing the separation of powers in the Constitution.

Through the years, I have often quoted a warning by Supreme Court Justice Louis Brandeis that resonates throughout a study of American history. It is especially relevant now:

> Experience should teach us to be most on our guard to protect liberty when the government's purposes are beneficent. Men born to freedom are naturally alert to repel invasion of their liberty by evil-minded rulers. The greatest dangers to liberty lurk in insidious encroachment by men of zeal, well-meaning but without understanding.

Brandeis's warning was part of his dissent in the first wiretapping case, *Olmstead v. the United States* (1928). The year before, in a less often quoted but even more profound definition of the spirit that has enabled this country to remain the freest in the world—despite severe misunderstandings of the Constitution by past administrations—Justice Brandeis again spoke to us now.

The case, *Whitney v. California*, concerned the prosecution of Charlotte Anita Whitney for violating the Criminal Syndication Act of California. That law, as constitutional scholar Louis Fisher noted, penalized "efforts of trade union and industrial workers to gain control of production through general strikes, sabotage, violence, or other criminal means."

Whitney "was found guilty of having organized and participated in a group assembled to advocate, teach, aid, and abet criminal syndicalism." In 1919, at a convention in Oakland, California, held to organize a California branch of the Communist Labor Party, Charlotte Whitney, as a member of the Resolutions Committee, signed this statement: "The Communist Labor Party proclaims and insists that the capture of political power, locally or nationally by the revolutionary working class, can be of tremendous assistance to the workers in their struggle for emancipation."

The Supreme Court upheld California's Criminal Syndication Act. But, in a concurring opinion, which was really a dissent, Brandeis wrote:

> A State is ordinarily denied the power to prohibit the dissemination of social, economic, and political doctrine [even though] a vast majority of its citizens believes [it] to be false and fraught with evil consequence ... It is ... always open to Americans to challenge a law abridging free speech and assembly by showing that there was no emergency justifying [its abridgement.]

That is precisely what the continually growing number of Bill of Rights Defense Committees around the nation are doing in challenging the USA PATRIOT Act and the other violations of the Bill of

Rights by Ashcroft and Bush. However, what Brandeis also said in *Whitney v. California* underlines this book's celebration of the gathering resistance to the war on the Bill of Rights:

> Those who won our independence . . . believed that the greatest menace to freedom is an inert people . . . They knew that order cannot be secured merely through fear of punishment for its infraction . . . that fear breeds repression; that repression breeds hate; that hate menaces stable government . . .
>
> Believing in the power of reason as applied through public discussion, they eschewed silence coerced by law—the argument of force in its worst form . . .
>
> Fear of serious injury cannot alone justify suppression of free speech and assembly. Men feared witches and burnt women [as in the Salem witchcraft trials] . . .
>
> *Those who won our independence by revolution were not cowards . . . They did not exalt order at the cost of liberty.* (Emphasis added.)

The challenge to Americans now is to act with the determination of those who won our independence because what we do now to recover the Bill of Rights will decide for years to come—as Justice William Brennan used to say—whether those words "will come off the page and into the very lives of the American people."

CHAPTER THIRTY-TWO

In the Enduring Spirit of Sam Adams

On September 19, 2001, Paul McMasters—the First Amendment Ombudsman for the First Amendment Center, who monitors the degree to which the citizenry is being informed on issues vital to their constitutional rights—issued an urgent message to the media, "Freedom Flees in Terror From Sept. 11 Disaster":

> Last Tuesday's terrors were so calamitous that they threaten to shake us loose from our constitutional mooring. A civil liberties catastrophe looms as citizens surrender to fear, fury, and frustration, and as lawmakers throw money and shards of the Bill of Rights at the specter of terrorism.
>
> Some of our elected leaders predict a gloomy future for freedom. "We're in a new world where we have to rebalance freedom and security," said House Democratic Minority Leader Richard A. Gephardt, Democrat-Missouri. "We're not going to have the openness and freedom we have had."
>
> Senate Minority Leader Trent Lott, Republican-Mississippi, repeated the warning: 'When you're in this type of conflict, civil liberties are treated differently.'
>
> Even staunch First Amendment advocates, haunted by the suffering and devastation in New York City, near Washington, D.C., and [in] the Pennsylvania countryside, are tempted to temporize in the face of insistent calls to suspend or re-examine our commitment to civil liberties . . .
>
> Fire from the skies and hatred from afar last Tuesday

caused human carnage and suffering at an unthinkable level. They dealt terrifying blows to our financial institutions, our transportation and communications systems, our political and military nerve centers, and to a nation's sense of self and security.

Paul McMasters ended his column: "Do we really want to add constitutional freedoms to that sorrowful list of casualties?"

He told me that for a long time, there was no response to that question from people in the media, and in colleges and universities, with whom he regularly communicates. But, as I've reported in this book, an answer to whether enough citizens insist that the Constitution remain as the ultimate bulwark to their individual liberties has indeed been rising from towns and cities throughout the country.

More of us recognize the naked truth of what Stephen Chapman of the *Chicago Tribune* says to all who will hear: "Liberty wasn't guaranteed by the Constitution. It was only given a chance."

Insisting on revivifying that chance, on May 6, 2003, the commissioners of Broward County, Florida, in a unanimous vote, passed the one hundredth local resolution in the United States, proclaiming their jurisdiction a "civil liberties safe zone." As Nancy Talanian, director of the Bill of Rights Defense Committee—which began this contemporary version of the Sam Adams–Thomas Jefferson Committees of Correspondence—says, "A civil liberties zone is a locale whose local government has passed a resolution declaring its commitment to protect the civil liberties of its residents."

On the same day that Broward Country became the one hundredth freedom zone, it was joined by San Mateo County, Marin County, and Sausalito, all in California.

Hawaii's state legislature finally passed the first statewide resolution on April 25, 2003, and Alaska and New Mexico followed.

As Nancy Talanian points out,

It took a year for the first fifty locales to pass resolutions; the next fifty took just two months. A movement that started in (generally liberal) communities has come to

143

include many more mainstream communities—including Tucson and Flagstaff, Arizona; Dillon and Missoula, Montana; Blount Country, Tennessee; and Minneapolis, Minnesota . . .

The growing movement of cities, towns, counties, and states clearly shows that when people look into the issue, they decide that they are not willing to surrender their liberties to the executive branch in the unlikely event that it might make them a little safer. Local governments recognize that real safety includes recognizing their residents' freedom of speech and assembly, rights of due process of law and to a speedy and public trial, and protection from unreasonable searches and seizures, without regard to the residents' citizenship.

Accordingly, the more than a hundred rededications to the Constitution around the country—across the political spectrum—contain in their proclamations, Talanian notes, "A government entity to actively monitor the implementation of the USA PATRIOT Act; any new such legislation, any new executive orders, or COINTELPRO-type surveillance and infiltration regulations. And to report regularly and publicly the extent to, and manner in which, local or state employees have acted under the USA PATRIOT Act and new executive orders."

In addition, these resolutions, all across the country, tell the federal legislators from these communities "to actively work for the repeal of those (laws and executive orders) that violate the guaranteed civil liberties enumerated in the Bill of Rights."

A fitting, and indeed roaring, American freedom fighter in this book is longtime Republican Representative-at-Large Don Young of Alaska. A former tugboat captain who accurately describes himself as "not one of these smooth, namby-pamby politicians," Young is a social conservative, a champion of Native American causes and of wildlife refuges.

During a radio interview in Alaska, on February 11, 2003, this plainspoken conservative said to a caller from Hooper Bay, Alaska,

"The events of September 11, as horrendous and horrible as they were, have had an even more horrendous effect—in my opinion and I think in the opinion of a lot of Americans—on our rights, through such of the legislation that has been passed as the USA PATRIOT Act. The worst act we ever passed."

"Did you vote for it?" the caller asked.

"Everybody voted for it," Don Young said, "but it was stupid. It was what you call 'emotional voting.' We didn't follow it through, we didn't study it. I think you're going to see—what I call—improvements, changes. . . . I say this very strongly. American citizens have constitutional rights, and we have to follow them."

On the National Day of Prayer, May 1, 2003, Attorney General John Ashcroft declared in Washington: "It is faith and prayer that are the sources of this nation's strength."

In view of Ashcroft's systematic invasions of our liberties, it is understandable that he missed the quintessential source of this nation's strength—the Bill of Rights—as Don Young of Alaska and increasing millions of Americans know, and are insistent on protecting.

CHAPTER THIRTY-THREE

Justice Denied at Its Source

The clear lesson is that the government, in its understandable and laudable resolve to protect our security, cannot be relied on to protect our basic rights and liberties.

—Lawrence Goldman, president of the National Association of Criminal Defense Lawyers, responding to the Justice Department inspector general's report on the post-9/11 mass imprisonment of immigrants with roots in this country

We did not violate the law.

—Attorney General John Ashcroft, testifying before the House Judiciary Committee, June 5, 2003

For all the growing rebellion around the country against Ashcroft's contorting of the Constitution, the conduct of his office has been most severely attacked so far by the June 2, 2003, report of Glenn A. Fine, inspector general of Ashcroft's own Department of Justice.

As usual, most of the media did not stay on this story long, but the inspector general's stingingly detailed internal exposure of Ashcroft's reckless disregard of the Bill of Rights has finally aroused enough congressional disquiet among more Democrats, and some Republicans, to lead to more sustained congressional oversight over not only the attorney general's sweeping, reckless violations of due process in the dragnet arrests and imprisonments (not just "detentions") in the months after 9/11, but also his insistence—during his June 5 testimony from the House Judiciary Committee—on demanding even more extractions of parts of the Bill of Rights.

During that testimony, Democratic Representative William Delahunt of Massachusetts went beyond the inspector general's report to echo the apprehensions of, by now, millions of Americans about Ashcroft's further intentions on violating their privacy:

It appears that the American people feel that the government is intent on prying into every nook and cranny of people's lives, while at the same time doing all it can to block access to government information that would inform the American people about what is being done in their name.

Delahunt's desire for open government includes his support of television cameras in federal courtrooms; and with regard to aberrant prosecutors, in and out of the Justice Department, he has worked with a bipartisan coalition to involve more DNA technology in the judicial process to prevent wrong but irreversible applications of the death penalty.

Ashcroft, in his appearance before the House Judiciary Committee, enthusiastically called for expanded death penalty sentences for those involved in terrorism that leads to fatalities. Like "material support" of terrorists, which he'd like even more loosely defined?

As for Inspector General Glenn Fine's report, the essence of his extensive evidence against the attorney general is that Ashcroft and some of the members of his senior staff deliberately established a policy that, as *New York Times* legal affairs reporter Adam Liptak noted on June 3, 2003—quoting the report—replaced "ordinary rules" with "no rules or perverse ones . . .

"The report says that the usual presumptions of the legal system were turned upside down in the aftermath of the attacks on September 11, 2001. As a result, people detained on immigration charges were *considered guilty until proved innocent* and often held for months [without bail] after they were ordered [by judges] released [or deported]." (Emphasis added.)

As you will see in chapter 35, in view of Ashcroft's indifference to, and ignorance of, certain highly relevant constitutional precedents during his conversations with senior officials of his staff during the days after the 9/11 attack, his approval and pursuit of this policy underlines his unfitness for office then—and certainly since. Those conversations are in Steven Brill's *After: How America Confronted the September 12 Era* (Simon and Schuster, 2003).

When I called the Justice Department to congratulate Inspector General Fine for his independence as an official whistleblower, I told his spokesman, Paul Martin, of what I had found in *After*. "We are familiar," said Martin, "with Mr. Brill's book."

It is useful to note that Fine is not an appointee of Ashcroft's biggest booster, George W. Bush. He was named inspector general of the Justice Department by President Clinton in 2000. (See, I can say something positive about the man who now, so some say, would like to be secretary general of the UN. He couldn't be any less effective than Kofi Annan. But Clinton too, as president, was tone deaf to civil liberties.)

As the inspector general emphasizes, hundreds of people, not yet "cleared" by the FBI, and therefore presumed innocent of links to terrorism under our former system of law, were imprisoned for weeks and months—"many in extremely restrictive conditions of confinement." In the Bureau of Prisons Metropolitan Detention Center in Brooklyn, says the report, these conditions included "'lockdown' for at least twenty-three hours per day; escort procedures that included a 'four-man hold' with handcuffs, leg irons, and heavy chains any time the detainees were moved outside their cells; and a limit of one legal telephone call per week and one social call per month."

Two lights were on in the cells of these "detainees" twenty-four hours a day, and some were slammed against walls by the guards. Moreover, the report points out that Justice Department officials admitted to the office of the inspector general that soon after the roundups started, they realized that "many in the group of . . . detainees were not connected to the attacks or terrorism."

Not one of the "detainees" in those roundups was at last ever charged with a terrorism-related crime. And, as you'll see in the next chapter, many prisoners were deliberately prevented from actually reaching attorneys.

Yet, as the *Times* reported on June 3, 2003, the inspector general's report refuses to "single out for criticism Attorney General Ashcroft or specific senior department advisers, prosecutors, or FBI agents."

In a message to Inspector General Fine, I asked how could he *not* criticize these serial Justice Department abusers of the basic human rights and civil liberties of all those unjustly maltreated prisoners. Fine has not yet given me an answer.

However, John Ashcroft's spokeswoman, Barbara Comstock, declares: "We make no apologies for finding every legal way possible to protect the American public from future terrorist attacks."

Where was the Congressional oversight?

CHAPTER THIRTY-FOUR

Ashcroft in Conference

In the hours and days immediately following [the September 11]
attacks, Attorney General John Ashcroft . . . directed that FBI
and INS agents question anyone they could find with a Muslim-
sounding name . . . In some areas . . . they simply looked for
names in the phone book . . . Anyone who could be held, even
on a minor violation of laws or immigration rules, was held
under a three-pronged strategy, fashioned by Ashcroft and a
close circle of Justice Department deputies including criminal
division chief Michael Chertoff, that was intended to exert maximum pressure on these detainees . . .

—from a summary of Ashcroft strategy sessions contained, in
further detail, in Steven Brill's *After: How America Confronted
the September 12 Era* (Simon and Schuster, 2003)

I came to respect Steven Brill's reporting skills years ago, when his
book exposed the scrofulous inner workings of *The Teamsters* (Simon
and Schuster, 1978). Since then, he founded *The American Lawyer* and
its chain of siblings, *Court TV*, and the now-defunct *Brill's Content*.
No longer associated with those influential stimuli to the media, Brill
is now a columnist for *Newsweek*. He returned to reporting in his current book, *After*, which—with clear source notes—lets us in on strategy sessions at the Justice Department in the weeks after 9/11.

These revelations add further critical weight to the June 3, 2003,
report by the Justice Department's inspector general, which, in my
view, powerfully questions Ashcroft's fitness for office—let alone his
subsequent USA PATRIOT Act and executive orders. The report was
based on internal documents and more than one hundred inter-
views with detainees and government officials.

In fairness to Brill, he does not agree with my assessment of
Ashcroft, specifically the attorney general's roundup of hundreds of

detainees whom he kept in prison for weeks, sometimes months, often under very harsh conditions, by turning the American rule of law upside down. Under his orders, they were presumed guilty until proved innocent. But Steve Brill told the *New York Times* (June 3, 2003):

> We have to acknowledge that we stood the system on its head. But maybe it was for a good reason. It was a national emergency. Ashcroft's view was that he would rather put 762 people away for some number of months if two or three of them are guilty or can prove some others are guilty.

Yet one New Jersey agent was justified in telling Brill: "I'm an educated person, not some bigoted Southern sheriff from the sixties."

A section in *After*, "Saturday, September 29, 2001" (starting on page 145), is based, says Brill in the source notes, on accounts from "two of the people who are closest to Ashcroft and were directly involved in these discussions (in the Justice Department)." The material is further confirmed, Brill adds, "by a White House official familiar with Ashcroft's articulation of the strategy in White House meetings."

Central in formulating this strategy was Michael Chertoff, assistant attorney general in charge of the criminal division. Recently, Chertoff has been confirmed by the Senate, eighty-eight to one, for a seat on the Third Circuit Court of Appeals (a level directly below the Supreme Court). Senator Pat Leahy (Democrat, Vermont) said he merited the honor of a unanimous vote. The one opposing vote was from Senator Hillary Clinton, Democrat of New York, because Chertoff was the lead lawyer in a Senate probe of the Whitewater affair.

You decide, from what follows, whether Michael Chertoff is fit to be a federal appellate judge. Worth keeping in mind is what Democratic Congresswoman Linda Sanchez said during John Ashcroft's June 5, 2003, testimony before the House Judiciary Committee. She skeptically asked the attorney general to comment on a pledge she says was made during the roundup of immigrants by Chertoff that "every one of the detainees has the right to counsel, and every one of the detainees has the right to make phone calls to attorneys."

The attorney general did not respond to her request for an answer.

In his book *After*, Steven Brill reports that in the strategy sessions at the Justice Department, Chertoff, agreeing that the detainees should be held for long periods of questioning, said that even if some got a hearing, "the hearings could not only be done in secret, but also could be delayed, and that even after the hearings were held and they were ordered deported [only for usually minor immigration violations], there was nothing in the law that said they absolutely had to be deported immediately. They could be held still longer."

As for the detainees' right to contact lawyers, Chertoff and the others in the room, reports Brill, knew that under INS rules, the prisoners "were entitled to call a lawyer from jail, but the lists the INS provided of available lawyers *invariably had phone numbers that were not in service.*" (Emphasis added.)

Brill adds that "according to one person who says he was there, someone in the room remarked that the government should not try too hard to make sure these people could contact lawyers. 'Let's not make it so they can get Johnnie Cochran on the phone,' another lawyer added."

In view of the many reports from families of detainees who were able to get lawyers (many were not), and from the lawyers themselves, there was indeed a deliberate, pervasive blocking of detainees' right to phone lawyers. And those orders, as Brill's book reveals, came from the top. At the very top, next to Ashcroft, was Michael Chertoff.

From page 148 of *After*: "Chertoff reasoned that while they were being held they would be discouraged from calling lawyers and could be questioned without lawyers present *because* they were not being charged with any crime." (Emphasis added.) *All these imprisoned were presumed guilty until proved innocent, as if they were in Zimbabwe, China, or Cuba.*

Months later, at the House Judiciary Committee hearing at which John Ashcroft testified, the ranking minority member, John Conyers of Michigan, accused him and the Bush administration of assuming "the . . . role of legislator, prosecutor, judge, and jury."

Unaffected by this charge, the attorney general claimed, in his testimony, that the president does have the power to arrest citizens on any American street, designate them "enemy combatants," and imprison them indefinitely, without access to lawyers or their families.

After all, Ashcroft said, "The last time I looked at September 11, an American street was a war zone." So, all of us, not just aliens in America, can become the disappeared.

The Justice Department still will not name the "detainees" in the previous roundup. It's necessary, said Ashcroft, "to protect their privacy." As for the inspector general's report, Ashcroft said he had "no apologies" for the dragnet roundup of the "detainees."

CHAPTER THIRTY-FIVE

The Once and Former Rule of Law

Despite the Justice Department inspector general's precisely detailed account of deliberate, pervasive violations of the rights and liberties of hundreds imprisoned by John Ashcroft in the wake of 9/11, neither the inspector general nor anyone else has spoken of bringing any civil rights or civil liberties charges against the attorney general and those of his senior officials responsible for these constitutional offenses.

If any member of Congress should ever begin to consider seriously examining the attorney general's qualifications for his office—which begin with his knowledge of the Constitution—I submit a passage from Steven Brill's *After*.

The revelation is in a section based on Ashcroft's haste, as soon as possible after 9/11, to push the USA PATRIOT Act through Congress. The White House, Brill reports, was concerned because Ashcroft had been in such a hurry that he hadn't first consulted even Republicans in Congress about the bill before it was sent to that body. Nor had the bill yet been circulated and "scrubbed" by the White House staff. Brill explains:

> Beyond his predilection to control as much as he could, some on his own staff thought that another reason Ashcroft hadn't "scrubbed" the bill beforehand was that he didn't appreciate the significance of the prosecutor-written laundry list he was proposing.
>
> Although Ashcroft is a graduate of the highly regarded University of Chicago Law School and a former Missouri state attorney general, even some of his own deputies [in the Justice Department] were surprised by how uninterested he was in the niceties of law.

Brill's sources for the startling information that follows are "two senators, one a Republican, the other a Democrat, [and] one veteran Justice Department senior lawyer":

> One veteran staffer recalls that throughout six different meetings on this bill and on another key legal initiative, he had never once heard Ashcroft cite a legal case ... Two senators—one a conservative Republican, the other a moderate Democrat—who spoke with Ashcroft at about this time were surprised at his lack of command of the basic issues. Whether it was lack of interest or lack of intellectual firepower, the attorney general seemed not to appreciate the complexities of the constitutional issues he was dealing with.

I have watched, on c-span, the attorney general's appearances before Congressional committees, and while he often insists that everything the Justice Department has done in the name of security is "within the bounds of the Constitution," he seldom cites Supreme Court precedents. When he does, he neglects the full context of the decisions which could cast doubt on the validity of his quick conclusions. The chief law enforcement officer of the United States need not be a constitutional scholar, but this attorney general's deficiencies in the essential tools of his trade were especially evident, as *After* shows, when they were sorely needed in those weeks after 9/11 when he was rushing through Congress the PATRIOT Act—the final version of which many members of Congress later said they hadn't time to read.

It could be illuminating if, at a hearing, Democratic Senator Patrick Leahy of Vermont, the ranking minority member of the Judiciary Committee, were to—without advance notice—give the attorney general a spot examination on the Bill of Rights. How *does* he interpret the Fourth Amendment ("The right of the people to be secure in their persons, houses, papers, and effects, against unreasonable searches and seizures")?

And the Fifth Amendment's guarantee of "due process of law"?

I would also greatly welcome the attorney general's reactions to a fundamental definition of Americanism by the late, extraordinary paladin of the Bill of Rights, attorney Edward Bennett Williams. In his *One Man's Freedom* (Atheneum, 1962), which demands to be reprinted, especially now, Williams described our most essential bulwark, as individual Americans, against overreaching government power:

> By civil liberties, I mean an individual's immunity from governmental oppression. A society which respects civil liberty realizes that the freedom of its people is built, in large part, upon their privacy. The Bill of Rights, in the eyes of its framers, was a catalogue of immunities, not a schedule of claims.
>
> It was, in other words, a Bill of Liberties. The immunities defined in this Bill of Liberties were set forth in order that the promise of individual freedom might be made explicit. The framers dreamed that if their hope were codified, man's energies of mind and spirit might be released from fear.

John Ashcroft's reign as attorney general has instilled fear not only among immigrants here, many of them with long, deep roots and families in this country, but also among citizens across the political spectrum, who have organized the more than one hundred Bill of Rights Defense Committees to safeguard themselves and their communities against *Ashcroft*!

Meanwhile, is anyone in the national government going to do anything about this fact—not just a charge—cited on the Jim Lehrer *NewsHour* (June 3, 2003) by Anthony Romero, executive director of the American Civil Liberties Union:

> Videotapes that were taken of the immigrants in detention . . . to safeguard against their abuse . . . were destroyed contrary to a policy that was meant to keep these videotapes indefinitely, *all of this coming from the Justice Department itself.* (Emphasis added.)

And over the last eighteen months we have heard from Justice Department officials insisting that they have done nothing wrong and they continue to assert that even though their own Justice Department [inspector general's report] asserts otherwise ... [a 198-page] report that documents fully the level of abuses and changes of policies that trampled on the rights of immigrants.

"That," he fairly shouts, "is not an ACLU report. It's a Justice Department report!"

When will Congress rid us of this despoiler of the Constitution?

Epilogue

The country needs to be born again.

—Margaret Fuller (1810–50), author, feminist, social reformer, editor of the Transcendentalist magazine the *Dial*, and associate of Ralph Waldo Emerson and the Concord Circle

Writing of the Justice Department inspector general's report on John Ashcroft's reckless dismantling of the Bill of Rights in the months after the September 11 terrorist attacks, *Washington Post* columnist Richard Cohen wrote (June 10, 2003): "The attorney general is far more dangerous than any of the immigrants he wrongly detained."

As this book has demonstrated, in cumulative detail, this is not hyperbole. When I have spoken since 9/11 to students and librarians, I tell them of the letter that Justice William O. Douglas once wrote to a group of young lawyers. It bears repeating:

> The Constitution and the Bill of Rights were designed to get Government off the backs of the people—all the people. Those great documents . . . guarantee to us all the rights to personal and spiritual self-fulfillment. But that guarantee is not self-executing.
>
> As nightfall does not come all at once, neither does oppression. In both instances, there is a twilight when everything remains seemingly unchanged. And it is in such twilight that we all must be most aware of change in the air—however slight—lest we become unwitting victims of the darkness.

The changes in the air are not only far from slight, but they are ominous in view of what a current Supreme Court justice, Anthony Kennedy, has warned, as I've noted: "The Constitution needs renewal and understanding each generation, or else it's not going to last."

But the Constitution cannot be continually renewed unless enough Americans understand its crucial guarantees of personal liberties against an executive branch that eagerly and righteously keeps assuming powers that the Constitution mandates be shared with Congress and the judiciary.

Because of their own ignorance of those constitutional guarantees, John Ashcroft and his champion, George W. Bush, unwittingly have become increasingly effective educators of more and more Americans in why—as William O. Douglas emphasized—"The conscience of this nation is the Constitution."

If Sam Adams and Thomas Jefferson could be aware of the waves upon waves of resistance in towns and cities throughout the country to the darkening authoritarianism of the present government, they would, I believe, be reassured.

Acknowledgments

I am grateful for the generous continuing support—at my home paper, the *Village Voice*—of Don Forst, Karen Cook, Jessica Bellucci, and David Schneiderman. Also, the staff of the United Media Newspaper Syndicate, and Wes Pruden, editor of the *Washington Times*.

Among my fellow members of the present-day Committees of Correspondence: Tim Edgar and the other Washington and New York staff of the American Civil Liberties Union, as well as Jonathan Turley, Charles Levendovsky, Matt Rothschild (*The Progressive*), the essential Nancy Talanian (Bill of Rights Defense Committee), and David Carle of Senator Patrick Leahy's Washington office.

Invaluable are the leads and investigative reports from readers around the country.

Also invaluable is Judy Bindler of Type Quik, the extraordinarily conscientious typist of this manuscript.

And, of course, Dan Simon, the creator of Seven Stories Press, who continues the spirit of Sam Adams. Also, Tom McCarthy of Seven Stories.

Finally, the jazz musicians who, from the time when I was eleven, have exemplified for me the life force of freedom.

Index

NAT HENTOFF is a longtime civil liberties commentator. He has written books on education, civil rights, and jazz, among other topics. His column is published weekly in *The Village Voice,* which Hentoff joined in 1957. His column "Sweet Land of Liberty" is published weekly in the *Washington Times* and syndicated nationally. Prior to coming to the *Voice,* Hentoff worked as a columnist for the *Washington Post* and as a reporter for *The New Yorker.*

A Fulbright scholar who studied at the Sorbonne, graduated with honors from Northeastern University, and did graduate work at Harvard University, Hentoff has been recognized with a number of awards. These include the National Press Foundation Award for Distinguished Contributions to Journalism and the American Bar Association Certificate of Merit for Coverage of the Criminal Justice System, as well as the Thomas Szasz Award for Outstanding Contribution to the Cause of Civil Liberties, and the American Library Association Immroth Award for Intellectual Freedom. In 2001, Hentoff received the Lifetime Achievement Award from National Society of Newspaper Columnists. Most recently, he was selected first place winner in the NSNC General Interest category, becoming the first to receive the award and then win first place the following year. Twice a finalist for a Pulitzer Prize, Hentoff lives in New York City.

Peace Agitator: The Story of A. J. Muste
The New Equality
Call the Keeper
Our Children Are Dying
Onwards
A Doctor Among the Addicts
Hear Me Talkin' to Ya (with Nate Shapiro)
Journey into Jazz
A Political Life: The Education of John V. Lindsay
In the Country of Ourselves
State Secrets: Police Surveillance in America (with Paul Cowan
    and Nick Egleson)
The Jazz Life
Jazz Is
Does Anybody Give a Damn? Nat Hentoff on Education
*The First Freedom: The Tumultuous History of Free Speech
    in America*
Living the Bill of Rights
Speaking Freely: A Memoir
American Heroes In and Out of School
The Day They Came to Arrest the Book
Boston Boy: A Memoir
*John Cardinal O'Connor: At the Storm Center of a Changing
    American Catholic Church*
Blues for Charlie Darwin
The Man from Internal Affairs
*Free Speech for Me—But Not for Thee: How the American Left &
    Right Relentlessly Censor Each Other*
Listen to the Stories: Nat Hentoff on Jazz and Country Music
The Nat Hentoff Reader